The Insider's Guide to
Writing
for
Screen
and
Television

The Insider's Guide to
Writing
for
Screen
and
Television

RONALD B. TOBIAS

WRITER'S DIGEST BOOKS
CINCINNATI, OHIO

This hardcover edition of *The Insider's Guide to Writing for Screen and Television* features a "self-jacket" that eliminates the need for a separate dust jacket. It provides sturdy protection for your book while it saves paper, trees and energy.

Other fine Writer's Digest Books are available from your local bookstore or direct from the publisher.

01   00   99   98   97   5   4   3   2   1

Library of Congress Cataloging-in-Publication Data

Tobias, Ron.
    The insider's guide to writing for screen and television / Ronald B. Tobias.—1st ed.
        p.   cm.
    Includes index.
    ISBN 0-89879-717-9 (hardcover : alk. paper)
    1. Motion picture authorship. 2. Television authorship. I. Title.
PN1996.T58   1997
808.2'3—dc21   96-47740
                                                                    CIP

Edited by Jack Heffron and Roseann S. Biederman
Production edited by Kathleen Anne Brauer
Designed by Jannelle Schoonover

Dedication
To Valerie, Always

ACKNOWLEDGMENTS

A lot of people gave of their time and mind to help me write this book, and so I gratefully acknowledge their expertise, charm and wit. I thank not only the people I interviewed for the book but the others who were always on the lookout for me, and in particular: Wilda Rokos, Michael McCallum, Diane Kamp, Jeremy Lape, J.B. Thompson and Doris Davis (who, although she had nothing to do with this book, had everything to do with the last one).

ABOUT THE AUTHOR

Ronald B. Tobias has covered just about every base as a writer and rewriter for features and network television. His forty-plus credits extend from one of the longest running series on network television (*Lou Grant*) to one of the shortest (*Baker's Dozen*). His features include *The Sixth Seal*, the adaptation for *A Killing Affair* and the action-thriller *Ambush*.

He currently teaches screenwriting and film production at the film school at Montana State University where he writes and produces documentary films for PBS and The Discovery Channel.

The author of seven books of fiction and nonfiction, Tobias also wrote *Theme & Strategy*, part of the Elements of Fiction Writing series, and *Twenty Master Plots (and How to Build Them)*, both published by Writer's Digest Books.

CONTENTS

The very nicest thing Hollywood can possibly say to a writer is that he's too good to be only a writer.
    Raymond Chandler, 1945

▪ Chapter One ▪

Inside the Mind of a Hollywood Screenwriter

Anyone who knows how to play chess will understand how to write a screenplay. Most chess players (like myself) stumble from beginning to end. We don't know much, but we know enough to play. We move without really knowing what's going to happen down the board. Maybe we can see one or two moves ahead, and, if we can, we're pleased by our uncanny ability to see even that far ahead. Better than the days when we couldn't see ahead at all—when we were playing blindly.

Over time, as we learned how to play chess, we made a startling revelation: chess depends more upon strategy than upon tactics. And we'd been happy with really short-sighted tactics. Suddenly we became aware of something called "The Big Picture." We began to see the game as a whole, not just a series of individual moves. And once we saw the game as a whole, we began to see patterns emerge in the play. Gambits, they call them. And the patterns have names, such as openings, middle games and endgames.

In chess, as in writing, the more you play, the more pointless blind play becomes. You're in it for coordinated, thoughtful play, a new complexity that brings depth and character to the game. These stratagems connect the parts to a whole, and *these connections in thought make the game.* No longer do you move randomly from point to point: Now you understand for the first time the concepts of purpose and direction.

What keeps the game from getting predictable or stale? The twist, the unexpected shift, the surprise departure from the pattern. Play the game long enough and either you give up or you realize that predictability is a short cut to defeat. And, as Laurence Fishburne's character in *Searching for Bobby Fischer* pointed out to his young student, in order to win you must play the player, not the board. So it is with screenwriting.

Most writers I know work in a vacuum. They work in places and states of mind far removed from a world that is very particular about the rules of its game. Some writers don't care, and that's fine. If you want to write a poem or a novel and you don't care how it's going to play in Peoria, then that's a conscious decision you make. I know writers who actually disdain the thought of an audience. Good writers, but not widely read ones. They think of writing as pure art.

By writing a screenplay, however, you accept the notion of writing for a large audience. While a blockbuster novel may sell half a million copies, a blockbuster film will reach tens of millions—even hundreds of millions—of people. I don't know anyone who reads screenplays for pleasure: Screenplays are written for the screen. They're the first step in a series of steps in making films. It isn't like a novel, short story or poem which reaches its final form in print.

Understanding this concept is critical to a screenwriter. It doesn't mean you have to cater to the "boob taste" of the movie-going public. It doesn't mean you have to write stories with the lowest common denominator in order to satisfy the largest number of people. That's playing the board blindly. What it does mean is that you have to understand the nature of the process of writing a screenplay. It means you have to know how to play a middle game and an endgame if you want to succeed in bringing your story to the screen. Tactics *and* strategy.

The point of this book is to present the whole. Once you understand the interrelationships among the various people who work to make a film, you can learn to talk to them in their own language. You can learn to write a story that does what it needs to do for the producer, director, actor, even the cinematographer and editor. They're the game pieces; you control the board.

It's your move.

EVERY SCREENWRITER'S NIGHTMARE

You can't cross a county line anywhere in America without hearing at least one story about a local nobody who wrote a first screenplay and then sold it to Hollywood for really big bucks.

A friend who's a veteran screenwriter likes to tell of the time he was hanging out at the Road Kill Cafe in McLeod, Montana, and struck up a conversation with a woman at the bar. (McLeod is one of those mini-havens from Hollywood: Within a thirty-mile radius you'll find getaway homes of at least twenty major Hollywood actors and producers.) The woman was new to the area, and, as you might guess, newcomers stand out in McLeod. When she asked him the inevitable question, "What do you do?" he confessed he was a screenwriter.

"Really!" she exclaimed. "I'm writing a screenplay too."

You and ten million other people, thought my friend as he prepared himself for the inevitable pitch.

She told him she used to work as a secretary at the CIA, and while she was there she got a terrific idea and sent it directly to Jeffrey Katzenberg, then the head of Disney Studios.

Any screenwriter worth a pinch of salt already sees the red flag: You don't send an idea to the head of Disney, especially some kind of espionage-spy thing; and even if you did, the head of Disney wouldn't read it. The script would be back on your desk the day after you sent it.

Anyway, she continued her already improbable story: Jeffrey loved it (screenwriters are on a first name basis with everyone in the universe) and said he wanted to buy it but thought she should have an agent, so he called Michael at CAA (Michael Ovitz, the head of Creative Artists Agency) and told him about her idea.

More red flags. You don't just call up the head of the most powerful agency in the United States and give away an idea. Anyway, the process was backwards: Agents call studio people about a property (that is, a script), not the reverse. This story was becoming too much to bear.

There was more. According to the woman, Michael loved it too and got her a million dollar advance based on nothing more than a partially complete script.

It was starting to look like a bullfight in Spain with all the red flags. *No one*, especially an unknown, gets a million dollars based on little more than an idea. The system just doesn't work that way. It doesn't matter who you are or how many scripts you've written.

Yet here she was, a former CIA secretary, light-years from Hollywood, sitting in the Road Kill Cafe and claiming she'd made a million dollars based on a pencil sketch.

Then she had the bold-faced audacity to ask my friend if he had any advice.

"Lady . . ." He reminded himself of his Southern reserve. "You made a million dollars based on an idea and you want *my* advice? *You should be giving it to me.*"

Maybe the story was true, although I doubt it. It doesn't really matter. What does matter is these stories are circulating, giving hope to a faceless legion of would-be screenwriters who think they can cash in on the big one. *If some half-baked ex-secretary from McLeod, Montana, can do it, well then, so can I.*

Let's talk reality.

Every year the Writer's Guild, the organization that acts as a clearinghouse for scriptwriters, registers about forty thousand scripts in the United States. Of those, less than half of one percent (about 160 scripts) actually get made into films. Not great odds, but definitely better odds than playing the lottery.

Still, who wants to put all the effort into writing a script only to have less than a one-percent chance of having it accepted? No sane person would expend that amount of time and effort on such a low probability of return.

The news isn't as bad as it sounds.

Two points are worth making:

POINT #1: The majority of people who write scripts are in it solely for the money. They aren't writers, they don't care about writing, and they haven't got a clue about how to go about writing a script.

When I say majority, I mean majority. I've been reading scripts for more years than I care to remember, and one fact overwhelms me: Eight out of ten people who write scripts haven't the faintest idea of how to go about writing one. I'm not talking about cosmetic aspects of writing such as format, either; I'm talking about the fundamental aspects of storytelling. These people are cluttering the script pipeline. They make life miserable for all the readers and agents who have to sort through this mess in order to find scripts that are worthy of consideration.

That's one way of saying that real competition—scripts that are well written by people who understand what a movie is—are in the minority. The bulk of those forty thousand scripts that are buckling the shelves at the Writer's Guild are a waste of human and natural resources. They've already arrived at their ultimate destination.

My advice to you is simple: If your motive is strictly financial, then reconsider. Play the lottery; your chances are better.

But if you like writing; if you care about telling a good story and want to write a script for the pleasure of it, then listen up. Your chances for getting a script produced have just improved greatly. Sure, money's a part of it—an important part—but it's not the primary motivation. Your primary motivation is that you love to write, you have a story to tell, and you'd like to see that story on the big screen.

A friend of mine who's a successful producer made a startling discovery about screenwriters. He said that whenever people found out who he was, they'd tell him that they were working on a screenplay. He'd be polite and listen and say things like "That's nice" and "Good luck."

It seemed to him that everyone in the state of California from the local carwash to the state legislature was writing a screenplay.

But then one day he was in a taxi and the cabbie pitched an idea at him. He liked the concept and asked to see the script. The cabbie suddenly faltered. "It's not ready yet." He started making excuses. "It needs a major rewrite." That's when my friend started challenging writers, and found out that, more often than not, all these would-be writers didn't have page one of a script. Everyone was working on one, but nobody actually had one.

The reason may have been that a lot of people have a story they believe would make a great film, but they don't have the time, commitment, or courage to actually put words on paper. It's far easier to talk than to actually write. So don't let the talk discourage you. If you're going to write a screenplay, write it. Rise above the babbling crowd.

POINT #2: All right, you've gotten this far because you enjoy writing stories, and you want to write a screenplay. We've put the issue of money behind us (or at least until a later chapter).

The second most common reason scripts fail is because the writer doesn't understand what a film is and how it works. I'm not talking about things like creative structure either; I'm talking about the politics of writing, the strategic part of the game. Many, many writers simply don't do their homework and even though they have a good story they don't understand the political, social and economic realities that affect everything in a screenplay.

Let me give you an example.

Early in my screenwriting career, I wrote an action-adventure screenplay which had a great premise. The story pitched easily and in ten seconds I could capture the interest of anyone willing to listen.

What if, I suggested, the United States had secretly developed the technology to create earthquakes at will? (There is scientific evidence that this may be true.) And what if our government used this technology as a geo-political tool to control third-world countries?

Good concept. Lots of possibilities. A friend and I wrote the screenplay and immediately a major producer optioned it. He was beyond enthusiastic: the screenplay was well written, the characters were engaging, and the action, he said, "Boy, the action was something else." It was time to celebrate; we had a hot property on our hands.

Well, not exactly.

The producer rough-budgeted the script to get an idea of what it would cost to produce. At a time when the average Hollywood production ran about $15 million, our story was estimated at $27 million, nearly twice the average cost of a film.

Sure, why not? I had location shooting on an oil rig in the Gulf of Mexico, and in places as far apart as Hawaii, Colombia, Mexico, Russia, and Antarctica. The film had several earthquakes, a tidal wave, and a volcanic eruption. It even had an underwater submarine chase and shoot-out. It was a James Bond extravaganza but without James Bond.

We'd written the best screenplay we could. We made it exciting and full of intrigue. But we made one fatal error: We didn't pay attention to how much these things would cost when it came time to producing them. Our great idea died on the vine because no one was going to spend $27 million on such an action pig out. (To give you a sense of comparison, that same film would now cost $80 million or more. There are very few producers in the world who can command that kind of financial commitment.)

The script went on a shelf and has collected dust ever since. We wrote a good story. We did everything we were supposed to except for one critical flaw: No one had ever taught us how things work in the world of making movies. No one had ever given me an inside view of the workings of the industry so I could learn why some scenes or sequences are better than others.

This information is critical to success. You can be a wonderful writer and fail miserably as a screenwriter. Many of America's great writers went to Hollywood (either literally or figuratively) and flopped, including William Faulkner, F. Scott Fitzgerald, John Cheever, S.J. Perelman, Nelson Algren, and George S. Kaufman. (George Bernard Shaw, on the other hand, made a single foray into screenwriting with *Pygmalion*, and won an Academy Award for Best Screenplay in 1938.)

The faulty assumption is that a good fiction writer automatically makes a good scriptwriter. The view is naive. A fiction writer has limitless freedom to create anyone, at any place, at any time. A word costs nothing more than the ink it takes to put it on paper.

Film is a different medium with a constant stream of limitations in terms of people, places and time, with which the fiction writer never has to contend. Each word in a script costs money. An average page of a script contains about a hundred words and costs about $250,000 (or more) to produce. Therfore, a *single* word of script costs $2,500! To get two actors to stand together while one says "I really love you," will cost a Hollywood production company about $10,000. There are many variables, of course, but at the average rate of production today, that's what it'll cost. And the price is going up by the minute, the high-budget film *Waterworld* cost over a million dollars per page to produce.

A fiction writer has unlimited freedom of ideas; the screenwriter is bound by financial realities.

The screenwriter faces other realities as well, like political realities which deal with the interaction between the writer and other people critical to making a film: the producer, director, actors, cinematographer, agent, even the sound and set design people. Since most writing takes place in a vacuum, totally removed from the reality of filmmaking, it's easy to forget about these people, but a script must talk to each of them. Filmmaking is a collaborative art, and each person responsible for making it happen is looking for something different in a script. A screenwriter never talks to a single reader: You talk to a whole boatload of people, each of whom has different concerns. Every producer I've ever talked to says the same thing: Moviemaking is a business. You can try to divorce yourself from crass considerations and focus on the artistic elements of storytelling, but the truth is you can't escape. You may not care about the bottom line, but others do. The investment is big: money, people and time. And everyone wants a return on the investment.

A section of this book is devoted to giving you an inside look at what people expect and what they hope to find in a screenplay. Each of these people is critical to the process of filmmaking: the producer (the person who makes the decision to make your screenplay into a film), the director (who molds your material into a vision), the actor (who interprets your lines), and the cinematographer (who translates words into images). Each of these people sees a script in a different way; each of these people understands a script as a working document. You have to learn to talk to each of them and answer their questions about the form and content of your work.

If you don't know what you're doing, you can alienate them. This book will teach you the politics of filmmaking. You'll understand what you should and should not do when writing a screenplay. You'll understand where the lines are drawn, and then learn how, when and where you can cross them without alienating others.

Once you understand how to get along with all your co-workers, you'll write better scripts.

INSIDE THE INSIDE

This book has two main goals:

First, to give you a clear understanding of the creative components of a good screenplay. Second, to give you a clear understanding of the politics of creating a screenplay. You can't separate one from the other.

Writing well creatively depends upon writing well politically. It requires tactics and strategy.

Some of the politics of screenwriting are so bizarre you'll probably end up asking yourself if the people who make films are really sane. Some of the informal rules and regulations that govern success in screenwriting are so arbitrary you'd think they were invented by someone at the Mad Hatter's tea party. But, as everyone knows, you have to play by the rules of the game if you want to play.

Hollywood reminds me of a fortress besieged: Everyone outside is trying to get in, and everyone inside is trying to get out. But the Hollywood experience is definitely an insider's game. Hollywood has its own way of thinking, its own way of acting and its own language. If you don't understand the mindset and the language, then you're an outsider. The trick is that it's possible to walk the walk and talk the talk no matter who you are and where you live. Hollywood gauges you on whether or not you're hip.

You don't have to move to Los Angeles to be hip or to understand how to behave. Sure, you hear it all the time: You have to be where the action is to get anywhere in this business. That's not necessarily true. If you're the type who likes banging on doors, going to every imaginable kind of event and *schmoozing* (shooting the breeze), if you actually like hanging out and looking for that crack of daylight that is opportunity knocking, then Los Angeles may be for you. But if you're like most of us and you hate all that song and dance, if you'd rather stay home and write rather than go out and talk about writing, then L.A. is not for you.

The most basic truth about Los Angeles and the movie business is that it's 98 percent talk and 2 percent action. There's an incredible amount of talking going on. Endless talk about plans, hopes and dreams; endless talk about deals; and endless talk about money. Los Angeles is a city rampant with gossip, rumors, dialogues and monologues, pitches and chitchat. If talk were gold, then Los Angeles would be paved with it.

Some of us have grown tired of the *spiel* and we know it chapter and verse. We know its lure and we have learned (to some extent, anyway) how to leaven temptation with reality. It's the business of dreams and fantasies, after all, and those dreams and fantasies aren't limited to the screen. They start before the screenplay and continue long after the screenplay has been produced.

There was a time when you could sit down with a producer or a studio executive and get money based on an idea sketched out on a napkin. Those days are gone. The cost of doing business has gotten too high.

There was a time, not so long ago, when you could get a green-light (a go ahead) based on a story outline (called a treatment). Those days are pretty much gone too. (But not entirely: In 1995 New Line paid Joe Eszterhas, the most highly paid screenwriter in the business, four million dollars on the basis of a four-page treatment.)

For most of us, the only way you can get moving on an idea is with a completed script. The days of the *schmoozer*-writer are dying.

That's both good and bad news.

The good news is that it levels the playing field. The value of an idea is now placed more in the expression of that idea (the script) than in how well someone can pitch an idea over drinks at a trendy restaurant. You hear it all the time: "The script is everything. Without the script there's nothing. Everything starts and ends with the script." That means someone in Bozeman, Montana, or Crab Orchard, Tennessee, has as much chance of getting a script produced as a struggling valet/waitress/pool boy/writer in Los Angeles.

The bad news is that as writers we have to make the full commitment based on faith and speculation. Most beginning writers write on *spec* (speculation: writing a script without a contract or a promise of any payment) anyway so that's not such a big deal. The problem comes after you've done a script or two and you don't want to write more unless you have some sort of financial commitment up front.

That's the reality of the business. So it becomes even more important for you to do your homework in order to maximize your chances for success. You need to stack the odds in your favor as much as possible. Don't get me wrong; writing a screenplay (much the same as writing a novel or even a poem) is a crapshoot. You'll never know for sure whether or not it'll go anywhere. There are writers in Los Angeles who are rich from writing screenplays and have never had one actually make it to the screen. (Sound crazy? Stop looking for logic in an illogical world. You're through the looking glass now.) At one time, Jim Cash and Jack Epps, Jr. were perhaps the hottest screenwriters going, yet every one of the famous team's projects up to that point had died in development. (Only in Hollywood is it possible to be a successful failure.) Finally, in 1986, two of their scripts finally made it to the screen: *Legal Eagles* (with Robert Redford) and *Top Gun* (with Tom Cruise).

I don't know of a single screenwriter who hasn't had a project die in what we call "development hell." (Development hell is the graveyard of projects that never get finished for any number of reasons: lack of financing, production problems, personality conflicts, and so forth.) It's the way of this world. And yet, we continue to write, always bucking the odds, dead set on getting our work to the screen.

If you want to be successful as a screenwriter you need, like any craftsman, a certain set of tools. These tools include an ability to write well and an understanding of the milieu in which you've chosen to work. That milieu is Hollywood. (Hollywood here is defined in the broader sense as the two major film cities in the United States: Los Angeles and New York.) The more you understand the mind and consciousness of Hollywood, the more you'll understand how to write for it.

Chapter Two

Inside the Mind of Hollywood

Hollywood is a place of diverse (some might say perverse) opinion. Every minute of action that takes place in the industry is preceded—and followed by—ten thousand minutes of talk, which, in Hollywood, is its own form of action. And like any ocean, it has its currents and tides. The person who chooses to swim against them is either profoundly clever or willfully ignorant.

The difference between being clever or ignorant sometimes seems marginal, but there's at least one important difference between the two. The person who's ignorant isn't paying attention and will get swept out with the tide. The person who's being clever, on the other hand, knows exactly what's going on and chooses to swim against the current. It's a calculated risk that can either leave you stranded or land you in the right place at the right time.

What does paying attention mean? Every industry has what it calls "conventional wisdom." In Hollywood, conventional wisdom includes things like who's hot and who's not, who's buying, who's selling, who's available and who's locked up on a project. For the screenwriter, conventional wisdom holds court on what kind of scripts or what kind of genres are right for the market at the moment.

Conventional wisdom is an imperfect science at best. It wants desperately to be able to read fortunes, but it stumbles along, trying to maintain some shred of dignity. For the kind of money that executives are getting, you would think somebody could predict what was going to happen next in the industry. F. Scott Fitzgerald wrote, "Not half a dozen men have ever been able to keep the whole equation of pictures in their heads." Some people believe Fitzgerald was either being kind or foolish. William Goldman, celebrated author of such works as *The Princess Bride* and *Butch Cassidy and the Sundance Kid* was more blunt: "NOBODY KNOWS ANYTHING." The capitals are his. Who knows where the truth lies? I suspect Goldman is closer to the mark than Fitzgerald.

The true prophet on such matters, however, may be Elinor Glyn, an English novelist who was famous at the early part of this century for her potboiler, *Three Weeks*. Even the producers of early cinema knew that illicit sex would translate into good box office, and so they courted Glyn to come to Hollywood to write for the silver screen.

She arrived seventy years ago when Hollywood was still testing its legs. Producers were uncertain of the moviegoer's taste. What to produce next? A melodrama? Or a western? Somebody asked Glyn her opinion about what would sell, and she replied astutely, although I doubt to the satisfaction of those who were listening: "Whatever will make the most money."

William Goldman's caveat ("nobody knows anything") hasn't stopped anyone from trying, and everyday people parade forth on the lots and in the cafes and in boardrooms pretending to have found the Holy Grail.

That doesn't mean Hollywood is just a circus of fools. Far from it. The shrewdest people I've ever met are there. They're often as intelligent as they are beautiful and rich; they're quick on their feet and devoted to their craft. They work tirelessly trying to make their dream come true. Some succeed; most don't. But everyone listens to conventional wisdom. For within it are shreds of truth that are essential for the player.

Conventional wisdom holds court on such things as the right (and wrong) way to do things. For example, it states that if you want to write a screenplay, you should behave in a particular, prudent way. First, you should write your screenplay (but only after consulting the appropriate books on the proper way to do it), and then you should find an agent who likes your work well enough to represent it to the right people. Sounds like sage advice, and for a few, it works very well.

The willfully ignorant person pays no attention to conventional wisdom. She writes a story and then sends it off to Spielberg (return receipt requested) and then sits back and waits for the phone call. And if Spielberg doesn't want it, there's still Lucas or Zemeckis or maybe just send it to Harrison Ford—I mean, he won't be able to resist the role you've written for him, right? Hollywood loves people who take initiative, or does it? In a town in which form is just as important—if not more important—than content, there are lots of people who will gladly tell you, "You just don't do things that way." Bullheaded as ever, you figure: What do they know? I'm going to sell my screenplay *my way*.

I'm not going to say it'll never happen. Even a blind squirrel gets a nut now and then.

The profoundly clever person, on the other hand, listens carefully to conventional wisdom; like the ignorant person, you decide to take the road less traveled, but your moves are calculated, not blind. You're playing an angle, not just charging into the arena and expecting everyone to snap to attention because you've arrived. Perhaps you've decided your script is perfect for Spielberg, but you know better than to send him the script without first figuring out how to get his attention (or the attention of somebody in Amblin Entertainment). And if you can't figure out how to get it to Amblin then maybe you know somebody at Castle Rock (Rob Reiner) or Imagine (Ron Howard) or any one of the hundred other production companies that populate the industry.

Where can you learn this conventional wisdom? Some of it's easy to find in journals like the *Hollywood Reporter* and *Variety*. Some of it's found on the street in cities such as Los Angeles, New York, Dallas, Atlanta, Nashville and Seattle. You can get conventional wisdom from anyone who's active in the industry, from the Executive Producer down to the lowly PAs (Production Assistants) who often know more about what's happening than anyone else, because they're hungry for information and contacts and are busy soaking up everything there is to learn. (I recommend talking to PAs, not only because their eyes and ears are always open, but because they're very easy to approach.)

The newsstand is swamped with movie mags about the industry; buy an intelligent one and you'll learn important information. A few years ago, Michael Hausman, the producer of films such as *Places in the Heart*, *Amadeus*, *The Client*, and *Nobody's Fool*, complained to me that he hated the proliferation of magazines and television channels like E! that take the ordinary Joe "behind the scenes" and give away secrets about how movies are made. He said it robbed movies of their magic. His reasoning was that if magicians steadfastly refuse to give up the secrets of their trade, why should filmmakers demystify their craft?

He may be right. There was something magical about movies before we knew about miniatures, latex, and 3-D compositing. We would watch and wonder: *How did they do that?* Now we know because E! and HBO take us behind the scenes and show us exactly how things work. We're still in awe, but we're in awe of the technical expertise of stunt people and special effects experts. Our attention gets too easily diverted from the story and the characters.

But a screenwriter isn't just another schmoe in the audience. All of this inside information adds up to knowledge, and knowledge is power. Once you start learning *how* things are done, and once you start learning *who* does them, then you are beginning to understand the nature of conventional wisdom.

Of course everyone in Hollywood has his or her own take about how things should be done, and not all information can be trusted. Opinions are pandemic; everyone has one and each one is different. The producers, directors, actors and cinematographers who I interviewed for this book didn't always agree on the right way to write a screenplay. But collectively there is a common thread of thought shared amongst all those people. As you read the interviews you'll have to decide for yourself what to trust and what not to trust. But beneath the particulars, everyone in this book is on common ground, sharing conventional wisdom.

Any producer will tell you that there's no absolute way of doing anything in this industry. And that goes for whatever information you glean from this book. A lot of what's out there is still undiscovered country. You'll have to learn by trial and error what's on and off target. And even then there's no consistency in that information: What works today may not work tomorrow; and what failed yesterday may work tomorrow. As any comedian will tell you, timing is everything.

So the information in this book is part conventional wisdom and part unconventional wisdom. With it, you'll learn how to travel both the road well traveled and the road not taken.

GIVING THEM WHAT THEY WANT

The golden question on everybody's mind is "What do they want?"

Find the answer to this question, and you'll have the key to the industry.

Ask this question and people will either stare at you like you're speaking in tongues or they'll smile and give you pat answers like "whatever the public wants." Elinor Glyn's answer is true, but it's also glib. Don't be foolish enough to ask what the public wants because no one, not even the public, can answer that. What the public wants is based upon a daily evaluation of nationwide box-office receipts. If a romantic comedy is in the number one slot and is making big money, then that's translated to mean "This is what the public wants." For the moment, for that film, yes. It doesn't necessarily mean that the public has an abiding hunger for romantic comedies and that you should scurry to your word processor and start turning out a romantic comedy.

Another futile activity is to try to predict trends in the movie industry. I have known people who study the Hollywood market like it was the stock market, analyzing product supply and demand and trying to forecast what kind of swing the industry will take next.

The analyst, for example, believes in cycles. "Let's see," the analyst says, "the market is saturated with police crime dramas and horror films. There's been a distinct decline in the production of westerns and science fiction. Therefore the smart writer won't be writing what the market already has, but what the market will be wanting: westerns and science fiction."

The theory is that the writer should be ready when the market finally comes around. Once the industry decides it wants a certain genre, its demand is immediate, and only scripts that are finished and waiting will be the ones to be produced. No point in trying to get on the train once it's left the station.

There's a great deal of truth in what the analyst believes. The cycles are real. We move through very distinct cycles in our viewing tastes. This is even more pronounced in television. Basically there are a few set genres in prime-time television: the situation comedy and the action drama. The action drama usually is either about police, doctors, lawyers or cowboys. Situation comedies are usually about family situations.

At any given time on television, you may notice a lot of lawyer programs or police programs but no doctor programs or westerns. The genre at its apogee (the height of popularity) will eventually wane and give way to a genre that is in its perigee (the lowest point). For several years all the shows are about lawyers, and then suddenly they disappear and the tube is full of westerns. They come and they go.

If you're interested in the historical phases of genre television get *Watching TV: Four Decades of American Television* by Harry Castleman and Walter Podrazik (McGraw-Hill Paperbacks). which shows the schedules of programs since the early days of television. Follow the genre through the years and watch how they wax and wane. If there are no westerns on television now, you can safely bet they will return. The question is *when*.

In the late eighties, I'd tell students in scriptwriting workshops that smart money would be on writing western scripts. There'd been a long drought of westerns and their return was overdue. When *Silverado* came out I saw that as a sign that the western was coming back.

I was right. And I was wrong.

I was right that the western was coming back, but I was wrong because it was coming back so slowly. Over the decade westerns would make periodic appearances: the traditional silent tough guy western (*Unforgiven*), the wild boy western (*Young Guns*), a black western (*Posse*), an all woman western (*Bad Girls*), legendary westerns (*Tombstone, Wild Bill* and *Wyatt Earp*), a comic western (*Maverick*). Perhaps the gate opened for westerns when *Dances With Wolves* was released and proved to Hollywood that there was a rich vein worth exploring in westerns.

It's the blockbuster that opens the door to the genre. Clint Eastwood's *Unforgiven* and Kevin Costner's *Dances With Wolves* paved the way. They were seminal works. Once the powers-that-be realize that a western can make fifty million dollars or more at the box office, then one or two things happen. The first is that the original success is fated to have a sequel: parts I, II, III, *ad nauseam*. This is a blood-sucking technique whose only purpose is to ride the cash wave of the original show. *Very* rarely is a sequel as good as its predecessor. Fortunately we won't have to put up with *Unforgiven II* or *Dances With Wolves II*.

The second thing that happens is that the original success spawns similar films. A call goes out for similar scripts. The demand is immediate: Producers want those scripts *now*, not six months from now, not one month from now, but *today*. In any case, films that come along after the original ground-breaking film have to labor in its shadow. Comparisons are inevitable.

Being at the right place at the right time means a lot in this business. But, I don't recommend trying to second guess the market: You will likely go insane trying to understand what no one has ever been able to understand. As a writer you should concentrate on producing the best script you're capable of, even if it is out of vogue. But don't invest your time in a genre script that might not come back into fashion for five or ten years, *unless* you feel strongly that the power of your story is irresistible. To its credit, Hollywood almost always will make way for a first-class script.

So how can you get an insight into trends?

Anyone who's played the stock market knows the danger of trends. They begin, they start to skyrocket, and suddenly they fizzle. The dollar dictates. A film's fortunes are either made or broken during the first weekend. Box-office reports are almost instantaneous, and the fate of the film that opens on Friday is already decided by Monday morning.

No one's sitting in an office at one of the major studios saying, "Let's start making westerns." They may be willing to float a trial balloon and see how the public reacts, but in most cases, studios aren't particularly adventurous or visionary. Films have become too expensive; speculation has become too risky.

A writer should take the time to know what Hollywood is thinking and doing on any given day. One important way to understand Hollywood is to subscribe to the *Hollywood Reporter* (5055 Wilshire Boulevard, Los Angeles, California 90036 or call (213) 525-2000). Warning: It isn't cheap; a subscription costs around $175 a year. If you can't afford a subscription, see if your library carries it. The *Reporter* is a daily and it'll bring more information to your door than you probably want, but it contains valuable, timely, indispensable information about the doings of Hollywood. I'm not talking about the fluff that you find in the pages of *People* or any of the gaggle of fan mags that are devoted to the lives of Hollywood stars. *Hollywood Reporter* is concerned with the business of filmmaking.

Of particular interest is a weekly section called, plainly enough, "Film Production," which is published in each Tuesday's issue. In spite of its innocuous title, the staff of "Film Production" actively seeks information about films that are starting or ending production. Normally a production company will wait until it has publicity and clearances from legal advisors and publicity before it lets the word out that it's going to make a film. But *Hollywood Reporter* aggressively seeks out the information and lists it in its Tuesday column, which can take up as many as twenty pages of the issue.

What does that mean? The information is straight forward: name, address and telephone number of the production company, and the names of significant participants, in front of and behind the camera.

The section also contains an overview for the week, listing the number of films in preparation, the number of films in production, the number of films moving into post production and finally the number of films being released. It also compares these figures with the same time period for the previous two years.

These figures are instructive. For example, the number of films in production is usually about *half* (though sometimes more and sometimes less) the number of films that are in preparation. That means every other film dies somewhere between preparation and production. Maybe the funding falls apart; maybe there are irreconcilable creative differences; maybe any number of things occur that keep a project from getting off the ground. (Actually the failure rate is much higher; this is just the ratio of films reported in the magazine.)

I don't read these figures to get depressed. I read the listings to find out who's doing what. You can tell the kinds of films that people are planning to make or are actually being made by their titles and the other information in the listing. That means you get a snapshot of the industry for the week. Are they making westerns? If so, how many? More than last month or last year? Do you see any trend developing? The listings aren't totally reliable indicators about what kinds of trends (if any) are developing, but it's the best information we have. Reading "Film Production" is like reading the market quotations in the *Wall Street Journal*; the facts are there—it's up to you to interpret them.

You can glean other kinds of information from the listings as well. You can tell who's hot and who's not. If a producer has two or three films in pre-production, then you know he has solid financial backing (which means he's in demand). You can tell which actors are up and coming and which ones have gone over the top. You can tell which studios are turning out product and which aren't. This information isn't spelled out for you; you have to read between the lines. But it's all there. All it takes is practice.

Let's say you have an idea that you think is perfect for a particular producer or director or actor. If you take the time to look at "Film Production," you'll know if that person's already busy with other projects (and consequently won't be "looking" for other work). Films in pre-production take, on the average, about a year before they're ready to be released into theaters. (A film can make it out in three months, but that's pushing it hard.) So "Film Production" gives you a sense of what's going to be in the theaters a year from now. A look into the future.

Conversely, if that person isn't busy with anything at the moment, he or she is "between projects," and may indeed be "looking for a property." That's the person you want to move on. Like I said, timing. Knowing when to make your move. Blind luck doesn't cut it. Information is power.

The *Hollywood Reporter* also lists television production for the week. If your interest is in the television market, then you'll find these listings equally valuable. In addition the Tuesday issue lists *Billboard* top twenties for albums, singles, video rentals, and video sales.

Another publication worth looking at is *Variety* (5700 Wilshire Boulevard, Suite 120, Los Angeles, California 90036). It also provides a section called the "Production Chart" which gives the same basic information as the *Hollywood Reporter*.

Both these publications often publish listings of all the companies actively engaged in television production. This information gives you names and telephone numbers of important contacts. Direct lines of information. You'll never know when you want to talk to a story editor of a particular show and find out if they use freelance writers or accept unsolicited scripts.

HOW CAN I GET INSIDE?

Don't stand in line. The line goes around the block, around the world, and you're at the end of it. You won't live long enough to see the front of the line. People will always be cutting in ahead of you. The line gets longer, not shorter.

So, you need to cut in ahead of all those who are standing in line.

There are a thousand ways to cut in. The actual number is limited only by the degree of your resourcefulness. Producers, directors, agents, studio people will all tell you pretty much the same thing: In effect, get in line. Write a script, send it to your agent, let your agent shop it around. Neat and convenient and boring.

The first rule of getting inside is to get noticed. You'd think that in order to get noticed you'd have to be in Los Angeles or New York. That's not the case. Sometimes I think it's an advantage *not* to be in the Big Apple or the Big Orange.

Why? Knocking on doors doesn't do it. (Sometimes it does, but numerically your chances are slim.) The establishment is so used to people knocking on their doors that they've set up a system of barricades to protect themselves from the door knockers. The first line of defense is the person who answers the telephone, whose job it is to keep you away from the powers-that-be. That line of defense also includes the receptionist inside the door. She might be polite and even nice to you, but her job is to keep the hordes back. It's like trying to attack a fort at the point of its thickest defense. You're not going to get through (unless you're incredibly lucky). You can't march in to Amblin Entertainment, announce yourself, and say you'd like to set up a meeting with Mr. Spielberg. If you try it, you'll get the stock response: "Mr. Spielberg is a busy man. Please leave your name, and a local address with a copy of your resume and someone will get back to you."

The person who's supposed to get back to you is the second line of defense. His or her job is to filter again. And so on and so forth. Even if Amblin Entertainment did end up hiring you, you might never meet Spielberg.

Conventional wisdom is that the greatest virtue anyone can have in this business isn't talent, it's persistence. You can't pick up an interview with someone at the top of the heap and not read the line somewhere in the interview, "I refused to give up. Things were looking awful but I refused to give up." Remember the beginning of *Wall Street*? A young, aggressive Bud Fox (played by Charlie Sheen) wants a meeting with Wall Street giant Gordon Gecko (played by Michael Douglas). He calls the front desk and asks for a meeting. He is refused. And refused. And refused. Finally Gordon Gecko agrees to meet Bud Fox after Fox has been told "no" thirty times. He's curious about this person who refuses to give up. The rest is history.

Banging your head against the wall may work sometimes, but there are other ways that are less painful. The point is, you shouldn't give up.

The test is just that: a test. A friend of mine who's an established writer with about ten books to her credit tells a story about a creative writing teacher who told her that she couldn't write worth spit and should take up something else like homemaking. She was so dejected she quit writing for years. Eventually, however, she returned to writing because its allure was too irresistible. She's done well ever since.

At face value it sounds like her professor did her an injustice by his cruelty, but he did provide one valuable service: He tested her dedication. If you give in because a person tells you that you're no good at it, then you don't really want to write. But if you've got your heart set on writing, then no one's going to stop you. Adversity challenges your will, that's all.

I used to make a game out of rejections. I collected them with a perverse pleasure. It was my way of dealing with the negative feelings that come with being told in a variety of ways everything from "Your work is wonderful and beautifully told, but we aren't accepting any more work," to "Your work is an insult to literature." (The rejection that hurts the worst isn't the insult but the one that comes oh, so close to being accepted. As I collected these rejections, I kept telling myself this was the hurt I had to go through in order to make it through to the other side.)

Well, I did make it through to the other side, and I started getting acceptances, and soon I forgot the drawer full of rejections. I don't know what happened to them, although I wish I still had them so I could look back and remind myself that yes, it is the process you have to go through, and you never fully escape its shadow. But persistence paid off. I was determined. And I finally got my break.

How do you get your break? If you can't knock on the front door, then where do you find the back door, the door that doesn't have all the muscle heads guarding it?

Forget the phone. Too many layers of protection between yourself and the person you want to get to. Use the mail.

Yes, a letter.

Several years ago, a student in my screenwriting course was crazy about a television show on the air at the time called *Matt Houston*. The show had been on for a few years and had decent ratings. She watched the show every week. She knew the characters inside out. And when the producers of the show took a right turn and started to move the character relationships in another direction, she wrote the producer a long letter critiquing the show in detail and explaining why she thought he'd made a big mistake with these turn of events.

Weeks went by and one night her phone rang.

"Is this Anna Eklund?" a voice inquired.

"Yes?" She suspected a salesman.

"This is the producer of *Matt Houston*. I got your letter and I think you hit the nail right on the head."

They talked for two hours. He was impressed by her insights and her articulateness. He said he would've liked for her to write a script for him but unfortunately the series was in its last season. No more scripts.

But he was moving on to another series as the producer. Would she be interested in moving to Los Angeles and working for him on his new series?

Anna was a single mother and had strong roots in her hometown. She turned the producer down. Meanwhile, Calvin Clements went on to become the producer of a hit show, *Dallas*.

▪ Chapter Three ▪

The Status of the Writer in Hollywood

You have an idea for a story, and you think it'd make a great film. Every writer begins with this conviction. If you don't believe in what you're doing, then no one else will either.

Perhaps the story is about something that happened to you or someone you know, and then again, maybe you just invented the story out of whole cloth. No problem. So you go out and buy some books that tell you the proper way to write a scene, a sequence, and an act. You learn about structure and things called plot points and backstory. Then you sit down and write the best story you know how. You don't worry about what things cost to produce. (Are you writing a $10 million film or a $100 million film?) You don't worry whether you're creating an appropriate star vehicle. (Do you have competing lead characters or does your story showcase a single actor?) You don't worry about any of the 1,001 political, social, and economic concerns that constitute a film. After all, you reason, those things are the producer's worries, not yours. All you need to concern yourself with is writing the best story you know how. Then, the rest will follow. Right?

Well, maybe.

Some of the people interviewed for this book think you would be naive to ignore the production realities of filmmaking. These people are sophisticated and thoughtful masters of their trade. And yet other interviewees think that it's a waste of the writer's time to worry about the mechanics of making a film. To do so, they reason, distracts the writer from the real purpose at hand.

Who's right?

Yes, you could write an Academy Award winning screenplay without any knowledge of or concern for demographics or production realities. It's happened before and it'll happen again. But is such an opportunity realistic?

Perhaps the best way to answer the question is to give an example. Joe Eszterhas—in the words of his agent, Arnold Rifkin of the William Morris Agency—"is a self-contained industry of creative ideas that capture the minds and imagination of the consumer." His movies have grossed over a *billion* dollars. Films such as *Basic Instinct*, *Flashdance*, *Sliver*, and *Showgirls*. That makes Joe Eszterhas one of the most sought-after writers in Hollywood.

His earning power is legendary: New Line Cinema paid him $4 million for *One Night Stand*. He sold the screenplay to *Savoy* for $3.5 million, and he made another $3.4 million for *Foreplay*. All this in about a year. Writer/director Tom McGuane made the observation that writers won't get any respect and more importantly they will never get any real power until they get salaries that are in line with what major actors and directors are getting. Joe Eszterhas is a case in point.

There are those who think Eszterhas is a script machine, that he panders to the market based upon his keen sense of what the public likes. Maybe. But what few people don't know about Joe Eszterhas is that he steps off the gravy train now and then and writes a story that he feels passionate about. In 1995, Eszterhas wrote a screenplay entitled *Blaze of Glory* about the relationship between rock-and-roll king Otis Redding and his manager, Phil Walden, during the civil rights movement. Given the strength of Eszterhas' name, his agent (then at ICM) put the script up for bids at auction.

The auction went for three days. The selling price?

Zip. Not a single producer made a bid for *Blaze of Glory*.

Why?

It's not that the man can't write. Everyone agreed the story was well written, the characters were engaging, and so forth and so on, *but*—and this was the deal-breaker—the script went unsold because no one thought the idea was commercially viable. In English, that means the producers felt that the movie wouldn't make back the cash outlay it would take to produce it.

Joe Eszterhas was sanguine about the rebuff: "If a writer believes in the story he's telling, it shouldn't be relevant whether it sells or not," he told *The Hollywood Reporter*. This wasn't the first time an Eszterhas script went unsold at an auction either; it was the *fourth*.

All right, if you're making $5 million a year selling scripts, maybe it doesn't matter if one of your scripts sells or not. The rest of us aren't nearly so philosophical about rejection. Contrary to his somewhat glib statement that it doesn't matter if a work sells or not, we do write with the expectation of having an audience, and if we write a film, then we write with the admittedly optimistic belief that our script has a shot—however long—at getting made into a film. Otherwise, we'd be writing Elizabethan sonnets or haiku.

Was Mr. Eszterhas foolish? Of course not. He wrote the story he wanted to write, and the cost didn't matter to him. You have to respect that kind of dedication. But at the same time you still have to be prepared to make the sacrifice of time and energy if the producers don't find your script "commercially viable."

If the odds don't matter to you, and you have a story you're going to tell come hell or high water, then tell it. There'll be passion and commitment in the telling, and that more than any other commodity is the most valuable element in a screenplay.

That vitality is essential to good writing. If you think you're cagey enough to put your finger smack on the demographic pulse of the American movie-going public, no amount of business sense will help you write better. You have to believe in what you're writing in order to make it convincing. This quality is the real foundation for a good script.

Without this foundation, it wouldn't matter if your budget came in under $100,000. A bad film is a bad film, even if it is a cheap one. (We should note that bad films are made every day, but that isn't always the fault of the scriptwriter.)

It would be foolish for you to read the trade magazines and decide upon a formula to pursue. "I want to write a screenplay that would budget for $3 million with a strong female lead," and then try to formulate a plot to go with it. That's mechanical thinking and it leads to soulless writing. You're not writing, you're prospecting.

If, however, you have a story in your head and you want to develop your idea with an eye towards increasing your chances for production, then that's just good sense.

THE SCREENWRITER'S DILEMMA

The position of the writer in the hierarchy of power and money is probably more complicated and less secure than any other position in filmmaking.

Dudley Nichols, the Academy Award winning screenwriter of *Stagecoach*, *For Whom the Bell Tolls*, *The Bells of St. Mary's*, and *The Informer*, tried to tackle the problem of who and what the writer was in his 1946 essay, "The Machine From the God." His insights haven't lost any of their value in the last fifty years.

The writer of any consequence, Nichols said, has thoughts, feelings and prejudices of his own. He creates stories by sitting at the "wheel-and-throttle" of his imagination. "But suddenly he discovers that he no longer has a wheel or throttle; they were checked outside when he entered the studio gates."

The writer who wants full control of his or her work sticks with the printed word. The novel, the play, the short story, the poem. The author's voice (hence the word, "*author*-ity") has weight. We're interested in what the author thinks and feels about his or her work, and we still defer to that voice.

The writer who writes for the screen, however, gives up that authority at the start. Instead, the writer is little more than the front end of a process that's more bureaucratic than artistic. "Indeed," wrote Nichols, "the artist is held to be a person never to be trusted to initiate a film; so the creative title of filmmaking is taken away from anyone suspected of being an artist and given to a man of more common taste who is called the producer."

In return for his or her compliance, the writer gets paid, by the standards of much of the world, a lot of money. In the eyes of Dudley Nichols and many other veterans, the purpose of this money is to buy out the writer's individuality and personality. "Every time [the writer] writes *bang-bang* or *I love you*, which is about all he is allowed to write except witticisms which have a mean edge to them because that is the only way his frustrated soul can now ease itself—in little bites at others—he marvels that millions of people who are hungry for pleasure and the great emotional and comic experiences of art . . ."

There's a cruel paradox for a writer at work here. It's a paradox a writer must accept in order to write for film. Wherever you go, producers, directors and actors are giving lip service to writers. (This shouldn't sound flip or cynical; in most cases, the speakers usually believe the compliments that they give to the writer.) To hear them speak, the writer is seated at Zeus' throne; all other things emanate from it. You hear producer after director after actor saying, "Without a script, you have nothing." Sounds great. But the praise is hollow. A better, more accurate metaphor would be to liken the screenwriter to a gas pump at a filling station. The automobile pulls up to the pump, fills its tank, and then leaves. The screenwriter is the gas pump, the script is the gas, and the movie production is the vehicle. The vehicle can't go without gas. Period. Nothing glamorous about that.

But who's driving the vehicle?

"The control of production is in a mysterious place called the front office," wrote Nichols. "It's in the hands of our modern demi-gods, the business men, who have never disciplined themselves for the sweat of writing, who have never created a character or a story, but who are very skillful at creating and running modern industrial organizations. . . ."

You should dispel romantic notions about being a scriptwriter. It's tough, demanding work. Financially rewarding, yes, but you pay a certain price for it too.

MONEY, POWER AND FAME

Julius Epstein, the co-writer of *Casablanca*, mused about the state of affairs for the writer today as compared to the way it was when he was writing. "In my day, we had screenwriters who were just as important as the hot writers of today. And they had just as much trouble keeping control over their work."

Larry Kasdan, the writer/director/actor, agrees that the writer is treated poorly in comparison to others. "If a movie's bad," he said, "[the critics] blame the writer. If it's good, they credit the director."

The fortunes of the writer over the years have remained relatively stable, however. "In an industry predicated on the daily calibration and reassessment of status and power," wrote Joan Didion, "screenwriters occupy a notably static place: even the most successful of them have no real power and therefore no real status."

Why are writers treated as second-class citizens, when everyone acknowledges that without a script, "even a ten-million-dollar actor couldn't get in five sentences?" Different people have their theories. One circulating among writers is that "the suits" harbor deep-seated resentment and jealousy for creative people. F. Scott Fitzgerald, after his experience in Hollywood, wrote a story called "Pat Hobby's Secret," in which a studio exec wishes that writers could be dispensed with altogether. "If only," he laments, "ideas could be plucked from the inexpensive air." Dudley Nichols concurs: "Almost every executive is determined to be a creator, and if he lacks any creative ideas or ability . . . then he will satisfy his creative urge by giving orders to men of creative capacity and so will create motion pictures by edict and sheer willpower."

Well, at this point in the development of technology, it looks like we're a lot closer to developing a computerized virtual actor than we are to developing a virtual writer. As much as the studio executives wish scripts would materialize out of thin air, they almost have their wish.

Thousands of writers are slaving at their machines on their own time at their own expense writing scripts for them. No risk, no charge. That comes about as close to free as I can imagine. There aren't too many people who work on speculation like that. Try to imagine doing your own job as a freelancer and being paid only if someone else found your work acceptable. Yet, we want it so badly that we take the risk.

Actually if there's anyone to blame for the current state of affairs, it's writers themselves. During the protracted writers' strike in 1988, writers who were out of work sat at home and stockpiled spec scripts. When the strike was over, a tidal wave of scripts flooded production offices, and the execs said to themselves, "Hey, why should I bother to pay for ten development deals with writers when I can buy one or two scripts that are already done?" So the market for spec scripts boomed. "This isn't an art," Fitzgerald's Pat Hobby exclaims, "it's a business."

The news isn't all bad. The trend is starting to reverse, and studios are going back to development deals. (For an explanation of a development deal and how they work, see chapter nine.) That means more jobs for writers. The studios may have had a sweet deal going for themselves, because the larder was filled with top quality scripts written by people who were out of work during the strike. Now, that supply has dried up, and the quality of spec scripts isn't what it used to be. Is the craze for spec scripts just a blip on the long-term scale? Time will tell.

One fact is certain, however, the writer who's motivated to create will do so no matter what the odds or how badly he or she is treated or paid. Power, fame and money are fringe benefits; the real payoff is the satisfaction of having your work on the screen seen by millions of people.

Hollywood has always counted on this fact.

Chapter Four

Inside the Director

Some writers labor under the unhappy delusion that those people in front of and behind the camera are in their service. They believe it's the director's responsibility to actualize the story they've created. These people are confusing a central issue. The people who work to bring a story to the screen are in service to the story, not the writer.

This is an important distinction to make. The script is the thing, not the writer. Of course, the writer produces the script, but the writer, however great his or her creativity, is only the first person in a long line of people who unify and create the vision which becomes a film. If you're a proprietary writer; if you feel you own every word you've written, and if you feel that everyone else owes you an obligation to realize the vision that you've conceived, then you should be writing fiction or poetry. The words of the novelist are preserved from beginning to end; no one steps into the process and adds another layer of interpretation. A screenwriter is a *writer*, not a filmmaker. You write words, but by virtue of writing words, you initiate a multilayered creative process of enormous proportions. Your script is only the first step in this complicated chain of events. To some extent, the screenwriter must learn to relinquish control. The only exception I can think of would be if you would write, produce, direct and act in your own film. Only then would you have complete control (and even that may be suspect). But the moment you let someone else into your film in any position, you allow another personal vision to enter the complicated creative equation that makes a movie.

When a director reads a script, he (or she) forms an image about what the story is about and how it will look. From that point, the writer is no longer the focus: The story is. The script now takes on another life, a life you cannot control. Complete control is yours only so long as the script is in your word processor. The value of the following interviews with directors is that both directors—very different types of directors—explain how they view a script in terms of filmmaking. Both directors also give us a tremendous insight into the actual mechanism of filmmaking itself—a mechanism that not only controls the writer, but everyone else connected with it. There's no such thing as complete control in making a film; there's only relative control. For a few brief, shining moments, each of us—the writer, the agent, the producer, the director, the actor—controls the film. But it is a transient moment, one that quickly and easily slips away.

An Interview With John McTiernan

John McTiernan's career includes not only box office smashes, but films that are seminal in the genre. His film *Die Hard* in 1988 virtually became the template for all action-adventure films thereafter, and his *Hunt for Red October* is considered one of the top cold-war films of all time. (McTiernan also directed *Die Hard: With a Vengeance*, a sequel that was so financially successful that the 1996 film season seems to have adopted the formula for all its films).

He also directed two Schwarzenegger films, the science fiction favorite *Predator* and the less-than-favorably received *The Last Action Hero*. The list of actors he's worked with is impressive: Sean Connery, James Earl Jones, Harrison Ford, Arnold Schwarzenegger and Bruce Willis to name a few. McTiernan is often characterized as an action-adventure director, a label he disputes. However he is characterized, few can dispute his talent or his success.

This interview gives valuable insight into how a director develops a script's character with principal actors. He also gives us a glimpse of how studio executives make their contributions to a production.

Tobias: Once you've read a script and begin to see your way through the story and the characters, how much license do you take with the script?

McTiernan: I'm pretty bad about deviating from the words on the page because I only view a script as a blueprint. It's written to be revised. The process is that you're making a movie, not photographing a screenplay. The screenplay is simply one of the tools you use to get there. It continually evolves as it confronts the experience and reality of making a film.

Tobias: What are some of the typical realities you encounter during the process of making a film?

McTiernan: There are many things in a screenplay that have values or meaning that may read well on the page but don't come off on film. It's great to have a studio executive understand a chain of dialogue on the page, but if you actually photographed it that way, it'd come off like a group of people talking in an extraordinarily expository way. So you punch holes in it and change it.

You also try to give actors room or push them to do their homework. One way you get them to realize character is to help them make the language their own and have it fit the scene they're working on. I encourage actors to shift dialogue. I keep track of what's important in the scene and make sure certain key lines get said. For instance, perhaps a certain piece of information needs to be ambiguous or shouldn't be overemphasized. My responsibility as director is to keep track of what the audience might think or know at a given moment.

Tobias: How do you know what's in the audience's mind at any given time? By watching the dailies or is it something you pick up in editing?

McTiernan: You can't necessarily even see it in the dailies. You keep it in your head. The movie is always evolving on the back of your eyelids. You keep track of where things are. At least you try to.

Tobias: Do you rewrite on the set?

McTiernan: Everything I shoot goes through my typewriter at least once. Most of my films go through all the colors of the revision pages two or three times, so that the final screenplay on the title page will have a stack of revisions. Usually I'll change dialogue or the way something is written because of the way I'm going to stage a scene. I always answer the question: "What does the audience learn in this scene?" Filmmaking is linear. There's only one piece of information on the screen at a time. And ambiguity is usually deadly. The audience needs to know what to think at any particular moment, even if it's wrong. So a screenplay has to have a schema of construction, a chain of information, if you will, of what information has to be delivered at each point in the story.

Exactly how that information will be rendered may change as you learn the actual circumstances of the filming. The writer rarely knows what the real physical surroundings look like or what the actors look or sound like. Even more so, a lot of times you find that the audience is ahead of where you thought it would be, so you have to adjust the information in a scene accordingly. Let's say you need to introduce a value or some information in a scene, but through no fault of your own it wound up in the scene before. Maybe it was just the way the actor looked that made it obvious to the audience what was happening. So the audience already knows what the script wants to say in the next scene. You can't say it again, so you take it out.

Tobias: Explain the process of revision from the point of view of the director and the studio.

McTiernan: The committee studio process of screenwriting has story executives or junior executives competing to call attention to themselves and thereby advance their career by "making a contribution" to a screenplay, particularly a movie that's "happening." So you end up with a lot of people volunteering at meetings. They say things like, "I don't understand this thing where he does such-and-such. That's confusing. We've got to fix that." What these people are really doing is showing off for their bosses. They're hoping somebody will notice them and say, "Hey, that's a sharp young kid. We ought to promote that person."

All of this information gets taken as the minutes of the meeting and then handed to the filmmaker. "You need this, you need that, blah, blah, blah." This usually only happens on big profile films because junior bozos won't invest energy in projects that aren't going to get made. The flies won't light on it, so to speak. In any case, the screenplay gets long and loaded with all sorts of nonsense such as long, rambling verbal explanations with lines like, "I'm going through this door now so I can speak to Bob about whether he spoke to Kathy last night." Just nonsense. You just have to weed that stuff out. Of course I'm overstating it in order to illustrate it.

Tobias: Can't you just nod to the executives when they offer you advice and say, "You're right, you're right" and then forget it?

McTiernan: Most of the executives aren't smart enough to know whether their line made it into the dailies or not. Or they've forgotten what it was. So you tell them, "It's a great idea," and the junior bozo thinks you're on his side. The next time he'll say, "God, that director's great. He's really on it," because he's figuring the two of you are building a lifelong alliance. But sometimes you have to go through the pantomime of shooting a scene or a line knowing all along it's going to fall through the cracks of the editing room.

Tobias: How do you encourage actors to find their way through a character? Do you do it at table readings or in rehearsals, or do you actually shoot it and see how it flies?

McTiernan: There's an axiom that no one actually pays attention until the camera starts rolling. So I try to schedule the first couple of weeks to be a space where the actor—particularly if he's a principal actor—can figure out what he's doing. You can't jump into the middle or tail end of a movie because by the time you go back and then return to where you were, you find you wouldn't have shot it that way. It'll stick out in the editing room and will look wrong.

The audience can spot this too. All of a sudden the audience will look at that actor and say, "This man suddenly doesn't know what he knew thirty seconds ago." There'll be something wrong in his face and his manner and in his eyes where he just doesn't know it. So it's a combination of table reading and some simple rehearsals if there are scenes that are primarily verbal. It gives everyone a chance to work out a few of the kinks and get started.

Tobias: What do you do if an actor wants to take his character in a direction that doesn't conform to your vision as director?

McTiernan: One of my jobs is to figure out how to take the contribution of all these people and fit it together and to know where their contribution helps and where it's neutral and doesn't hurt. If the actor comes up with something that does hurt, then you speak up. You just say, "Wait a minute. You realize if we do this, then when we get to such and such we'll be in trouble." I've never had an actor who didn't listen to that. But it's good that they have ideas. It means they're working on it. It means they care. It means they're paying attention.

Occasionally you'll get a younger actor who has some silly notion of what he wants to do. That's not hard to deal with. But with seasoned actors, the solution to your problem is in the original premise. They're experienced professionals. They didn't get to be a movie star by being stupid. They've worked with many directors who've made dozens of films. You can talk to people like that. If there's a problem, explain it.

Tobias: Are your films an expression of yourself as the director or of your actors?

McTiernan: I don't try to have everything in a movie be an expression of me. I don't love myself that much that I think I should be making movies entirely about me. A movie that has a lot of creators, that has ideas and thoughts and energy from a lot of people, will be a lot better. All I try to do is focus it, guide it, be the ringmaster, if you will. I'm a mirror and an advisor for an actor. I don't create his performance. I just try to put him in a space where he can perform. I've been fortunate in that I've worked with real professionals who knew what the hell they were doing. The last thing I want to do is tell them not to do it. I want to figure out how to use what they're bringing and have that contribute to the overall story.

Tobias: How would you characterize the state of Hollywood right now?

McTiernan: There's a wonderful line in *Bang the Drum Slowly* about the ball players who used to walk into a motel and con the locals by playing a card game they called TEGWAR, which stood for The Exciting Game Without Any Rules. It's a wonderful metaphor for the movie business. There are as many different ways of working out things as there are personalities and financial arrangements.

When Mario Kassar and Andrew Vajna began financing films with foreign pre-sales, they created a new way of doing business. They had to have an element such as a box-office name they could point to and say, "Here it is, up front. This actor will make the movie a hit." They couldn't do that with the strength of a script, so they had to bank on the strength of an actor's draw. I'm not saying that other people weren't doing it twenty years before, but at the time it was sort of a revolution. The studios hated it. You used to hear studio executives badmouthing Kassar and Vajna for how they were ruining the business. And the studio executives promptly began imitating it. Well, what they're doing is safe. Although safe in Andy and Mario's case is very different than safe in a studio's case. Andy and Mario have made their way through life by betting the whole bundle. But for a studio executive to take the safe route and only put proven talent in a film isn't particularly insightful or courageous.

Because the studios have been imitating what Andy and Mario were doing, they've created a five-fat-fish mentality for any project of any significant size. So you have to get Harrison or Arnold or Sly or Mel to be in it. It's made tremendous distortions in the content of movies, because you now have people competing to get movies made by attempting to attract one of these five or six thirty-five to fifty-year-old white male actors. Now there's an elaborate rewrite process that goes on with manuscripts that includes comments like, "He's just not heroic enough." And so now you find that in an awful lot of screenplays the subsidiary characters spend a tremendous amount of time talking about the main character. It's like it's the only thing on their mind. And it distorts the content of movies because only films that have this kind of starring role for the lone-wolf hero will advance. Obviously, there are other things to tell stories about.

Tobias: Now that some leading actors are getting twenty-million-dollar paychecks, how will that affect how films are made?

McTiernan: Some leading actors were always commanding huge salaries. They might have been disguised in other ways, but the costs were still there. Often with these people it's not the cost of the salary, it's the come-alongs and the friends and all the people you have to give associate producer titles to who get large fees for doing nothing. Maybe it's the buddy who's supposed to be a stunt coordinator but who's terrible and will make mistakes that will cost you two or three million. There's an awful lot of that stuff. It's unfortunate. Believe it or not, it's a lot easier to get $20 million for an actor than it is to get $1 million.

Tobias: With films like *Die Hard* and *Predator*, did the screenwriter conceptualize Bruce Willis or Arnold Schwarzenegger in the lead roles or were they added after the fact?

McTiernan: *Predator* was Larry Gordon's project. He put it together. Arnold was interested in doing it, so to some extent the script had to change to take advantage of what Arnold brings.

Tobias: Was that also true for *Last Action Hero*?

McTiernan: Yes, but in that case the studio started monkeying with the script *after* we started shooting. They sold the blanket in eleven directions. They'd convinced themselves that they had eleven different movies. They had an action movie, and they had a children's adventure, and it had to be PG-13, but it had to have action and violence and this and that in it. It was a confusion of intention or a lack of honesty about what we were doing from the beginning. To a certain extent some people never saw past the deal. "We've got a big actor, the big script, the big director, and we're going to spend a fortune on it . . . this is just going to be hot stuff."

Tobias: Do you think that confusion carried all the way through the film?

McTiernan: Absolutely, on the executive level. The movie that I and Arnold signed on to was a fairy godfather story, and the original notion was that this film was going to be rated PG-13, with no real violence in it. It's not about violence. It's about a kid with no father who finds one. It's literally Cinderella, plopped the other way around.

Tobias: Was it because Schwarzenegger is so tightly bound to violence in those kinds of roles that they won't let him divorce himself from it?

McTiernan: No, not at all. The studio wanted to sell this movie as the greatest thing since sliced bread, so it had to have everything in it. It can't seem to be what it is. So they began monkeying and working on Arnold after we were already shooting. They were rewriting behind my back. I'd hear whispers about new pages floating around; it was a nightmare. So it was pushing, trying to cram traditional action beats into the last third of the film after we already started off in one direction.

So to some extent we wound up with a movie that had either lost or changed its focus in the middle of making it. The intention on the filmmaker's part and on the star's part too was to go in one direction. The studio wanted to go in another. The essence of the problem was a certain intellectual dishonesty on the part of the studio executives involved in that.

Tobias: People were writing pages behind your back and giving them to the actors?

McTiernan: No, not to the actors. The idea was, "Well, we work on the pages and then we take them to McTiernan after we've decided that this is what we should be doing."

Tobias: Who was doing that, the studio executives . . .

McTiernan: . . . and the writers.

Tobias: So how do you feel about having writers on the set?

McTiernan: I feel great about it. I'm always trying to keep the writer on the set, or at least encourage him to stay. Usually you can't because he's off on some other job. They already got paid for this one and they're not going to make any more money if they hang around, so they're off on something else. And sometimes it's necessary to hire somebody else to hang around. We're continually calling the writer while he's off on another project, saying things like, "You know that scene where such and such happens? We need a line there. Bruce needs a line." I think there's something in "Die Hard" about a TV dinner. Bruce's character is in the duct and he says, "Now I know what a TV dinner feels like." Well, we're in the middle of shooting that and called the writer who was off at home working on something else, and said, "We need a line here. It's too good an opportunity."

Tobias: How much of Bruce Willis's lines are ad-libbed in the two *Die Hard* films you directed?

McTiernan: That's the way he works. It's got to come out of that space in his head that his character is in, and if an idea isn't coming out of that space, it's not going to be worth anything. You've got to give Bruce a chance to work, to go through the process he goes through to produce his best stuff that people find appealing about him. We're still talking about changes to screenplays—his particular manner, his work habits are utterly the opposite of say, Sean Connery's. Sean does his homework before he comes to the set. He wants to rehearse each scene a few days before, and he does his preparation at home. Then he comes to the set and it's there. It's finished. You'd better have the camera and other things worked out so that you catch his second take because that will be the best one. You better bloody well catch it.

Bruce is just the opposite. It's got to happen there in the here and now. He's got to know what the real things are and the real people and the real circumstance, and he's got to tear apart the scene, throw out every bit of dialogue and every bit of planning, and then gradually get back to it. And he arrives almost where you started, but he has to go through the destruction process or he'll never get there. Or if he gets there, he'll be flat. He'll be behaving like a good boy. And it's an emotional thing somewhere in there, because Bruce's stardom, the thing that's most appealing about him, is when he's throwing dead cats in other people's cathedrals. When he's breaking up crockery. And if he isn't breaking crockery, he's feeling like he's back in a Catholic school and he's got his tie on straight and he isn't screwing around. And all of a sudden he's not entertaining because he's being a good boy. You have to give him a chance to break things. Sometimes it's exasperating. Sometimes it's hard on everyone else, certainly on the filmmaker. Because you have to get it in your head that you're not really going to know how you're shooting this scene for a while. I'd have to consign some days or half-days to say, "Okay, let's work this out."

Tobias: Then you conform yourself to the work habits of your actors?

McTiernan: Of course I do.

Tobias: Where do you draw the line between the character as created by the writer and the character as created by the actor?

McTiernan: The actor is key to translating a part into reality. And I don't think it's a failing on the screenwriter's part either. The only time a writer should fill in with character background of more than just the main character is when the person's character has plot significance. For instance, at a crucial point in the third act, a person who the main character's been depending on is going to wimp out because we, the audience, have always known that the guy was basically a coward. That's plot significance. We've got to have that in. Occasionally you may have a problem with an actor confronting the reality that he's playing a nonessential character and so he wants to make his role significant, but it's best if you can get the actor to fill in the character work on his own. It won't come from the screenwriter.

Tobias: What are the screenwriter's basic responsibilities to the director?

McTiernan: Tell the story, period. The only time there should be any visual description is when it is relevant to the plot. The rest of it is just junk that will cause the reader to think this person isn't a professional.

And camera direction is nonsense. That's just a screenwriter trying to tell some executive he's really a director. All it really does is make the writer look like an amateur.

Tobias: What about nonvisual detail? Burt Leonard once bought a script for *The Naked City* because of the descriptive phrase, "He walked down the street with five thousand years of Jewish suffering on his face."

McTiernan: It's an extremely succinct, clear, intense description of character. The first beat of this movie is that there's a man on the street with five thousand years of Jewish suffering on his face. The photographer then has to translate it. His shoulders are stooped. There are lines over his forehead. His *peyos* are tied in tiny knots. His mouth turns down—you see what I mean? You could add bunches of detail that would amount to five thousand years of Jewish suffering. Let somebody else work out the specifics. There's nothing wrong with putting that sort of description in a script. That's wonderful when something like that shows up in a screenplay.

Tobias: Do you feel a minimalist approach to detail is the best way to write a screenplay?

McTiernan: Certainly I do. I'm rabid about minimalism. In my own rewrite I'll take out half the words in a screenplay. But that's for shooting, and I understand that to some extent you want more description and a clearer description experience for a studio executive, the buyer. But even there, the clearer you are about the story the better. Don't picture a mood with words. Get to it. Tell people what they need to know.

Tobias: Do you think it's wise or silly for a writer to write for a specific actor?

McTiernan: There's nothing wrong with it. The writer may have been right. Furthermore, if it's right for one of these thirty-five to fifty-year-old male lone-wolf hero characters, then it'll probably be right for one of the other ones. If Arnold isn't interested in it because he already did something similar two years ago, maybe one of the others is because he hasn't done something like that. But those movies are extraordinarily devoid of content. In some of those movies you really do have actors where it becomes not the filmmaker's medium but the actor's medium, and you have so much self-glorification. A tremendous amount of the movie is devoted to advertising the star, showing what an incredible commodity the star is. And the star usually isn't wrong in a business sense. The reason they're stars is that they learned at some point how to highjack a movie and make it appear to be about them. Now they quite explicitly will turn a movie into a commercial for the corporate enterprise known as Harrison Ford or Tom Cruise.

Tobias: Do you advise the writer to be concerned with the political, economic and social considerations of making movies when writing a script?

McTiernan: Not unless the writer is specifically working with a producer who is saying, "For economic reasons I need this to be a such-and-such." Of course it's possible to ignore economics to too great an extent when you're writing descriptions of things that may cost millions of dollars. Prudence says you should probably avoid that. But people who read the script won't notice those things. They're looking at story. If you have a good story, the other stuff will get worked out.

I went to school at the American Film Institute. The best thing they did was make us work on black-and-white videotape. They wouldn't let you get lost in the technology because what they gave you was so simple you couldn't possibly put much energy into it. Either you had a story to tell or you didn't. It was just as naked as possible. It was a wonderful decision on their part. Usually film school people are just lost in the hardware. It's a diversion. Because by the time you get the opportunity to use it, the hardware will have developed two or three generations. So, to some extent anyway, to worry about economics in a screenplay is missing the point and doing destructive things, because while you're involved in that you're not paying attention to finding the story.

Tobias: How can a writer learn about the true costs of making movies?

McTiernan: In so-called "large budget movies" you have everyone conspiring to spend more money. Everybody wants to spend more and build their portion of the budget. So rather than ending up with more filmmaking, you wind up with a bigger bureaucracy. And the person who's conspiring most to spend more money is the studio. Half their budgets are air. There are dollars that go back and forth inside, internal dollars. Phony dollars. Every time you're on a set and you need a longer cord for the telephone, it has to go through the studio bureaucracy, and I'll bet the movie will be billed $5,000 before you're finished for that longer cord. And if you try to do it on your own—like send your assistant and say, "Go down to the five and dime and buy one of those things"— you'll get reported and there'll be a big hassle about it because you spent $4.00 instead of $4,000, and they don't like that. Particularly for movies that they anticipate will be large revenues. They conspire like crazy to create the illusion of costs.

The other large lie that goes into budgets is independents who produce very expensive movies that they sell overseas. DeLaurentis was almost always making "the most expensive picture ever made." Who knows if he was spending $1.38. He'd tell everybody he just spent $40 million because he was trying to sell overseas on the basis of how much he has in it. That's another class of extraordinarily expensive movies that aren't necessary.

According to the studios, the only movie I've ever made that went into the black was *Medicine Man*. That's in profits. The original *Die Hard*—the one they scrambled all over themselves to make the third sequel—is officially in the negative. So is *The Hunt for Red October*.

Tobias: But nobody believes it for a second. It's just a paper charade, right?

McTiernan: Not a charade. Lying is the word. Lying. Theft.

Tobias: Do want to go on record as saying that?

McTiernan: Yes. I use those words specifically. It is theft.

Tobias: Tell us more about what constitutes a well-made story.

McTiernan: If you have a real story to tell, you won't be able to whittle it down. Description will fly at you. Everything will suggest a specific. If a person in your story has a specific role that comes out of his character, the nature of his character, if he commits actions that come out of his character, and if those actions come from or are of plot significance, then the specifics about what he looks like and how he sounds will almost be self-evident. It's only when you go into the other direction where you know what the guy looks like, what he sounds like and what he wears, but you don't know what he does, what he thinks, who he is, that description is useless. You're trying to intuit from the outside in, when you still don't know what function he performs in the story.

Tobias: Do you read coverage (a reader's summary of a script)?

McTiernan: Only occasionally. Most coverage is dreadful. If you find somebody who can recognize the essence of a story and put it in the coverage, that person is golden. Right now I don't have anyone with that skill, so I don't bother with coverage. What I will have is a conversation. I'll ask questions trying to lead to the essence of the story. Eventually I'll get it, but if I sent that same person off to write a two-page coverage, I'll get all of the salient specifics of the plot without knowing a damn thing about what the movie's about. There's a wonderful John Gardner line about the definition of insanity as pure facts in isolation robbed of their nuance.

Tobias: Do readers serve any purpose, then?

McTiernan: It's a great entry-level position and a wonderful training ground. It's like working in the delivery room at an agency. What do you learn? You learn who everybody is and where they are. You see how things come and go, what sort of things come and go, and you get a basic overview of the nature of the industry. Then you move on to your next job where you sit at the telephone. You're the secretary, the telephone operator for an agent, where you learn specifically how it's all done. Those are wonderful training environments. Reading could be too if institutional knowledge was there. But it's not. If you read the old coverage from back in the thirties, it's far more articulate, much more useful, because you're reading stuff from people with much better literary educations and much more training in how to identify the story. Coverage won't be a chain of what a person does. It'll be the essence of the story distilled down.

Tobias: Most readers don't have good critical and analytical skills?

McTiernan: The studios won't invest in training people to do that. And that's exactly what their executives need—the ability to analyze the essence of the story and where something does and does not work so they're not always trying to put Band-Aids on things.

Tobias: Should beginning writers concentrate on writing small budget films? Or should they go for the gold and write big budget films?

McTiernan: It depends on where they are. If they're out of Los Angeles, they should definitely write the smaller ones. If they're already a certain way along on their career and in Los Angeles they should write the expensive one. You should write movies that you would want to see made. Write honest stuff that has something to do with what you'd really like to see. And if it really has that quality, other people will see and notice it.

Tobias: Then you believe they should stick to what they know best to write about?

McTiernan: Which is another way of saying, "Write something that's honest." Half the stuff that gets written is a regurgitation of other movies that people have seen. There are so many things that exist as clichés that are just cycled through and through and through, over and over again. And it won't have anything to do with any reality that ever existed. It just has to do with other movies that people have seen. You see a tremendous amount of that.

Tobias: Then why do we see so many gimmick movies, movies made from old television shows and so forth?

McTiernan: The main thing that's wrong with most of Hollywood product is that it's barren. It's empty. Hollow. People are not in the business of telling stories, they're into writing deals. That's why they can make twelve movies in a row out of a 1950s TV series. That's a pretty clear definition of bankruptcy. You obviously haven't a thing on your mind other than to make a buck. They don't care. If it isn't movies, it's another commodity. It's just that movies offer the most money for whatever is available in their lives. Very, very seldom do you find one of them that knows or cares anything about movies. Which is why screenwriters and filmmakers have to subversively introduce and maintain story values.

Tobias: Do you sense a hunger in the audience . . .

McTiernan: Oh, absolutely. Time and again you'll see a movie that makes money for no reason other than the audience hasn't seen it three times in the last five years. It makes money for the sheer reason that it has honest content. Someone actually cared what it was about and spent more than fifteen minutes thinking about it. It isn't a photographed deal; it's a story.

Tobias: Is Hollywood amoral, then?

McTiernan: I view Hollywood as morally neutral. It doesn't give a damn one way or the other. It's a mechanism for making movies. I find making moral judgments on it a waste of time. I make moral judgments about my own behavior, but not about large systems that I can't change or that no group of people could change. Anyway, by the time you figure out how it works, it's changed.

If you said, "Okay, we're going to build the very best, most thoughtful version of Hollywood we possibly can," you'd wind up with some Stalinist nightmare. It can't be done. It's a weird market that fluctuates in a particular way at the moment, and five years from now it will function in some other way. The best you can do is attempt to have some sense of how it works.

Tobias: When studios or producers offer you a script, do you find that they only think of you as an "action" director?

McTiernan: It used to be that way. I certainly got 150 versions of *Die Hard* over the years. But now I see just about everything. But just as certain scripts get to make the rounds of acceptable actors, so scripts make the rounds of acceptable directors. John Milius talked about the hundreds of people surrounding a tank with five fat fish in it, and everyone is trying to get one of the fish to bite on his hook. Some movie companies will invest in certain filmmakers to use as bait for their hook.

If we have a script that we want to get made, we'll invest in that particular director because he'll help us get that particular fish and then we'll have our movie. It's a silly process.

Tobias: How do you cope with such a process?

McTiernan: You fashion a reasonable strategy through the game that gets you approximately what you want. I got to work on movies where I like the movie. I've never been forced to take a job because I needed a job. I try to live reasonably prudently and pay off my mortgage. From the time I was nineteen I decided I wanted to be a filmmaker. Until I was thirty-six, I never made any money at it. And when I did make some money, I'd put it back into being a filmmaker or trying to buy properties. I'm trying to keep that head now, so I can tell them off if I want to.

Tobias: That's a luxurious position.

McTiernan: It's an onerous one. You have to fight to get it. You have to fight your wife and don't let her spend money. You have to fight friends who say, "Don't you think we ought to start X, Y or Z business?" or "Don't you think we should have this big movie company where we'll take all this Japanese investment money and then we'll yaddah, yaddah, yaddah?" It's always smelled to me like, "Wait a minute. You could wind up moving from what you know how to do into what you don't know how to do. Or worse, you could wind up making a movie you don't like." We somehow get euchred into it. It's dangerous. That's why I won't live in Hollywood.

An Interview With Steven Soderbergh

In 1989 Steven Soderbergh blasted upon the scene with his first work, *sex, lies, and videotape*. The witty, intelligent film was a raw *tour de force*. It won the Palme d'Or at the Cannes Film Festival and the script was nominated for an Academy Award. To say he was a precocious filmmaker would've been an understatement.

Since then, Steven has made three other films, each very different from the others. In 1991 he made *Kafka*, followed by *King of the Hill* and *The Underneath*. He wrote the scripts for *sex, lies, and videotape*; *King of the Hill* and *The Underneath*, (although on the latter he used the pseudonym Sam Lowry to indicate his displeasure with the Writers Guild arbitration of credit).

Tobias: Compare your role as the writer and your role as the director on *sex, lies, and videotape*.

Soderbergh: Looking back, I would've done things differently. The fact that it was written and made very quickly ended up contributing to both its stengths and its weaknesses. Its strength came from the emotional momentum we built up, but its weakness was that I didn't have enough time to reflect upon the material and shape it more, write scenes further off the point than I did.

Tobias: Off point?

Soderbergh: There's the scene in which we first meet Peter Gallagher's character. He's talking on the phone to a friend of his saying, "When you get married and you've got this ring on your finger, women start running to you, and it's a great thing, and you're going to love it." It really doesn't make much sense that Peter's character would be opening up to anybody. What I think Peter's character should have done was to say, "Marriage is a great thing. I've gotten a lot out of it. It's really made me a more mature person." Etc., etc. And then three minutes later we see him go sleep with the sister.

Tobias: Did you feel the exposition was being dishonest?

Soderbergh: It was just too naked. There was no sub-text. It's only by trial and error that you learn these things. Editing is a great place to learn about redundancy and realizing how much doesn't need to be spoken or reiterated, what can be done with a good actor and what can be done with the placement of a camera to put points across.

You need to have a healthy disrespect for your own material. You have to be willing at any point in the process to throw out the scene or the story and start over, tear it down and say, "This doesn't work. We have to stop and come up with something better."

You learn to be open. It's a matter of receptivity, and it's not just restricted to writing. It could involve a piece of production design or a costume or a location—anything. But in general one has to be open to new and better ideas and willing to throw it out and start over again when an idea isn't interesting or isn't up to snuff.

My goal as director is to orchestrate as many accidents as possible and capture them. That's at odds with what a writer hopes to do when he or she sits down in front of a blank piece of paper. Personally, I hate writing. It's a terrible gig. I've only done it by default either because it was quicker and easier for me to do it instead of telling somebody what I wanted them to do, or I had something in mind that really did come out of my mind, so I figured I might as well sit down and do it. But I really don't enjoy it, and I would never do it for pleasure. I don't consider screenwriting to be writing per se.

Tobias: What is it, then?

Soderbergh: Screenwriting is fake writing. It's writing with pictures, and you can fake your way through a screenplay, but you can't fake your way through a novel. Of course there are exceptions—screenplays that read like self-contained literary works—but those are few and far between. In general, a screenplay is a way station between somebody's idea for a movie and the movie itself. I don't find it to be a very evocative format to write in.

I think the reason I hate writing so much and the reason I find it so hard is that when I'm not able to do it to my satisfaction, it's a very primal failure for me. Because what it means to me is the sum total of all that I have to draw upon is not enough. I don't know enough. I don't have enough experiences. I can't imagine enough. That's why I'm stuck. It's being dry in a very basic way that says you haven't been around long enough to figure this out. I hate that sensation, and whenever I write, I get it. That's what's terrifying about it to me.

I just turned in a rewrite to Miramax that I was really struggling with. I'd done a draft that I sent to the director, and he had a lot of notes. I was having real trouble coming up with a new draft. I finally got it done, but I was beating myself up because I didn't finish it on the schedule I had for myself. But when I finished it, I realized that it was better and different by the virtue of seven more days. I'd lived seven days more and somehow knew a little bit more than I had seven days earlier. Time passing, even in small amounts, can make a huge difference when you're writing. I wasn't physically or mentally capable of producing that script seven days earlier. Some life experience or some idea or whatever provided the solution. And I've learned, as hard as it is, not to push it. It'll come but you have to be patient.

Tobias: As a director, what do you mean when you say you need to orchestrate as many accidents as possible?

Soderbergh: It means giving freedom to everybody who's in a position of some creative importance on the film. It means creating an environment in which ideas are circulating and people are encouraged to put forth their ideas. It means keeping everything loose enough so that when accidents occur people understand not to shy away from them.

Tobias: Do you have any examples?

Soderbergh: Jeremy (Irons) is a very bright guy and a very creative actor. One of my favorite things in *Kafka* is the moment when everyone has gone to lunch and Jeremy's going through Alec Guinness's office, and he's looking through the drawers in his desk. Jeremy thought it would be funny to have a little danish with a bite taken out of it in one of the drawers, as though this guy, who's supposed to be a figure of great power and perfection, has this little thing he keeps hidden, a little danish in his drawer. I thought it was funny. It's a tiny thing, but if you add those up over the course of the movie, they can make a contribution. And you like everybody to make those sorts of contributions on all levels.

Tobias: Does it happen on all your films?

Soderbergh: It doesn't always happen. *Kafka* was a physically tough, demanding film to make. It was a long schedule and I was having a running battle with my director of photography. And it was a weird movie. Every day I had to try to figure out the tone of the movie. At key places the film lost its tone and its energy. I'd make the film very differently now. I would make it funnier, looser, and much more exuberant. The whole film is so maddeningly controlled, which certainly echoes the protagonist, but I don't think that's a good enough reason to be that controlled. I wish the experience of watching the film were more fun. I saw the whole thing as a fun-house ride. Unfortunately, it has the seriousness that a lot of films by young people have before they realize that the most grown-up thing you can do is make a really funny movie. A legitimately funny movie. As you grow older and take yourself less seriously, you realize that's a very honorable and wonderful thing to do.

Tobias: Are you hard on yourself?

Soderbergh: I am hard on myself. I'm also hard on other people. In terms of talking about one's own work, I don't understand the idea that you have to constantly present yourself and your work as being something that's really great. The level of critical discourse in this country is extraordinarily low, and it's because you don't see anybody talking honestly about their work, their motives for doing what they do, and how they feel about what they do and how they feel about what other people do. That's too bad. You see more of it in Europe.

Tobias: Have you ever engaged in honest discourse?

Soderbergh: When I did interviews on *The Underneath*, I didn't pretend I thought it was a great movie. I didn't pretend I liked it. I didn't want people not to go see it—because I thought it was worth seeing—but I couldn't sit there and say I thought it was as good a film as *King of the Hill*.

Tobias: Is *King of the Hill* your best film?

Soderbergh: It's the best normal movie I can make.

Tobias: Normal?

Soderbergh: By normal I mean narrative mainstream filmmaking, which I'm stepping out of into a more experimental, nonnarrative, nonlinear, perhaps unreleasable kind of filmmaking. For me it's a real return to what I started making as a kid. It's the result of a process I've been going through. I wasn't ready to handle that freedom until now. It took making *The Underneath* and having that be a miserable experience to put me down that path in a definitive fashion.

Tobias: What were the restrictions on your freedom that led to this?

Soderbergh: The language. The cinematic language that you have to use to make a film that is theoretically going to be seen in a large number of theaters by a large number of people.

Tobias: Is the denominator too common?

Soderbergh: Not really. It's just the same old over-the-shoulder shot, wide shot, people talking about plot. Just the things you have to do if you're going to make a normal movie.

Tobias: What freedoms do you seek as a filmmaker?

Soderbergh: The ability to follow any idea as far as I want. The freedom to show up on a location on a given day, look at what you've got, decide it's no good, pile all four of your crew members in the car, go eat lunch, talk about it, see another place to shoot on the way back from lunch, take everything over there and shoot something completely different that's better. It's an interaction of one's life and work that I used to have.

Tobias: Sounds like stream of consciousness.

Soderbergh: A lot of it is.

Tobias: So you're no longer making the traditional concessions to plot points and three-act structures?

Soderbergh: I find that too confining. At least right now. I may come back to that. I may come back to it with a new appreciation, but right now it's boring to me.

Tobias: Are you giving up structure in the traditional Aristotlean sense in order to explore character or . . .

Soderbergh: No, because even dreams, which have their own weird logic, also have structure. I think we inherently like to feel there's a point to what we're watching. But I don't think the points need to necessarily be made as clearly as they often are. Alan Rudolph (director, *Equinox*, *Love at Large*, *The Moderns*) called me after he saw *The Underneath* and said, "You know, the problem with the kind of films that you and I make is that they play better on the way home." People just aren't really as interested in that kind of movie experience as they used to be.

Tobias: You mean movies that make people think?

Soderbergh: Movies that when you reflect upon them have more to give you. A lot of people don't go to movies for that type of experience any more.

Tobias: Audiences seem not to tolerate any kind of ambiguity any more. They can't tolerate any kind of subtlety. Everything has to be crystal clear and repeated three times so even the dead would understand. Do you find that a restriction as well?

Soderbergh: The films I make are filled with ambiguity. As a result they've tested very poorly, and whether or not that's the reason they've also performed poorly, I don't know. The point is, though, even though I think by mainstream standards they're ambiguous, I don't think they're ambiguous enough.

Tobias: Who do you make films for?

Soderbergh: I please myself and then hope I please others. It's the only reference point I can trust. Otherwise, you're second guessing. That doesn't mean I don't get input from people around me, but the general thrust and central ideas have to interest me, and then I just hope. There are certain standards of quality that you should adhere to, but you should do the work that you love and please yourself.

Tobias: What was your relationship with Lem Dobbs (the screenwriter for *Kafka*) like?

Soderbergh: I would call it happily contentious. Lem is extremely bright and extremely opinionated. After the first screening of *Kafka* he sent me a nine-page, single-spaced fax that was one of the most brutal things I've ever read. I didn't agree with all of it, but I did with some of it. It didn't bother me in any real sense, because Lem has very high standards and very definite ideas about what's good and what's not.

Tobias: Was he present during filming?

Soderbergh: Yes. He told me what he liked, and he told me what he didn't like. I know there were certain casting choices he wasn't happy with. But at the same time he knew it was my movie ultimately and that I was going to do what I wanted to do.

Tobias: Do you like having the writer on the set?

Soderbergh: In some ways I wish Lem had been around more, and in certain areas I wished I would've listened more. It wasn't anything bothersome. I've done two episodes for Showtime's *Fallen Angels*. My friend Howard Rodman adapted both of my episodes and was around the whole time. I enjoyed that a lot. I think he did too.

Tobias: Do you encourage the writer to be present?

Soderbergh: It depends. If I felt he (or she) was going to be a destructive influence, I'd tell him to stay away. But if I felt he could make a contribution, then great.

Tobias: After your debut in 1989, you were besieged with scripts. In a general philosophical sense, are there things you despise seeing in a script?

Soderbergh: Just disgust at reading something that's stupid, something that aspires to nothing but a sale. That drives me crazy.

Tobias: When you say stupid, are you saying essentially they're devoid of any kind of intellectual concept or content?

Soderbergh: Its world view is pedestrian and unexceptional. The writer has no real interest in or sense of how people interact. Put those things together and that covers just about all the scripts you read. With some exceptions. I've read some very good things. I've read more good things than you'd think I would've read, and a lot of them I've liked but didn't want to make.

Tobias: How would you characterize the Hollywood mind-set?

Soderbergh: Hollywood seems to operate under the idea that if during a certain calendar year a studio made twenty movies and two of them were really, really good, then if they make forty movies next year, that four of them will be really good. I don't think it's true. In my opinion, there's a finite amount of truly great art that can exist in the world and that it doesn't increase exponentially when you increase the number of works being produced. I think there are five great movies out there in a year, whether thirty films are made or three hundred. Those five great films will emerge no matter what and they have nothing to do with the volume of bad films. But that's not the way Hollywood thinks.

Tobias: Your films have a strong central vision. Obviously that's important to you. Is that something you've actively realized intellectually? Do you find that it's one of the primary components of your filmmaking?

Soderbergh: Less so as I get older. There's a difference between immoral and amoral. A writer, I think, has to be amoral. He has to be able to argue and believe all sides of any issue and make an audience believe it. And I feel that if one is living a life that runs counter to that, you'll always make a movie in which the outcome of the argument has been decided before the movie is even started.

Tobias: Then you get your central tension from thesis and antithesis and running the two against each other so there is no clear outcome?

Soderbergh: I want to move further into that area, both in my life and my work. I'm not only tired of the structures of the normal filmmaking world, but I'm getting tired of the structures that I put around me in my life as well. As a result, I'm just dropping that and following whatever I feel like doing, wherever that may go. Sometimes it turns out well, sometimes it doesn't.

Tobias: Then getting between a rock and a hard place, where there is no clear or right solution, is the ultimate ambiguity.

Soderbergh: I think that's where we live. That bothers a lot of people. They can't live their life without more structure. Maybe five years from now I'll want that structure again. But right now I'm rejecting the norms on all levels.

Tobias: What is your goal as a filmmaker?

Soderbergh: My goal is to write a movie in which nobody ever says anything near what they think or want and in which all the significant activity occurs off screen. If I could write that script—and someday I think I'll be able to—that would be ideal for me. Pinter is like that when he's really cooking. His collaborations with Joseph Losey are masterpieces of subtext and subterranean motive. *The Servant, Accident*, and *The Go-Between* are great, great films.

Tobias: There's been the call for years for an evolved cinematic language.

Soderbergh: That's what's so great about the project I'm working on. The advances in film technology are leading toward being able to make movies this way. The stocks are fast. The lights are getting smaller and cooler and cheaper. You can buy very good old equipment for small amounts of money through clearinghouses. The sound equipment is better and smaller. Now you can make a really good movie with five people. It can't be a period piece, and the physicality of it is restricted by your ability to get people to do things for you for nothing. But it's all there. And yet nobody seems to be taking advantage.

Tobias: Do you think that's because everybody wants the big score?

Soderbergh: I don't know. I guess it comes down to why they got into making movies in the first place.

Tobias: Are you talking about a budget under a million dollars, under a half a million, or what?

Soderbergh: I'm talking about $75,000.

Tobias: Used car prices, in other words.

Soderbergh: Absolutely. You need to know how to make a movie from the ground up, because you have be the leader, you have to do everything yourself. That way you know if everybody is doing their job too. You can't just say, "I want to make a movie for seventy-five grand," hire four people to be your crew and sit back and watch. You have to be the guide. You've got to have the desire and the knowledge. Then you can make your own film.

Chapter Five

Inside the Actor

The question probably immediately arises in your mind: what does an actor have to do with how a writer creates a script? It's an important question that doesn't have an obvious or easy answer.

There are two reasons why a writer should understand the role of the actor. The first reason is political. The role of the actor in the production process has changed slowly since World War II, and those changes are more pronounced now than they ever were. Not knowing how the actor fits into the production process may create some pleasant—or nasty—surprises later on.

The second reason why a writer should understand the role of the actor is more profound. I've found that because most writers are kept out of the production process that they don't understand what an actor does. Well, you say, an actor *acts*, right? What's so difficult about that?

Acting is an elaborate interpretive process. So it's important for the writer to know what an actor is looking for in a script. Of course there's a wide variety of thinking among actors about how to act, but there are certain important common denominators that writers should know about the acting process that affect the script. A good writer can alienate an actor by the way he or she presents the character's material. This chapter will teach you how to write to and for an actor.

POLITICS AS USUAL

A few years ago I was doing some film work in what was then the Soviet Union. I was on the set of a motion picture watching a scene being shot in a medieval dungeon. I noticed a man standing behind the director who would occasionally bend over and whisper into his ear. I assumed he was a producer. I was wrong. He was the scriptwriter. In the Soviet Union, the last say belonged to the writer, not the director. Charlton Heston was quick to point out that might be the reason why the Soviet

Union hasn't produced any films of quality.

In the United States, the writer takes a different place in line. (This joke is an example: "Did you hear about the aspiring starlet who was so stupid that she slept with a screenwriter?") Directors seem to have all the creative power these days.

Or do they? Some people are suggesting that the power is slipping away from the directors and ending up with the A-list actors. Because certain actors have so much clout at the box office, and because Hollywood has gone to great lengths to coddle these people, they have begun to demand—and get—tremendous discretionary power. They can demand a certain director for a project. Or if the director is already attached to a project and the actor doesn't want the director anymore, then they can demand the director take a walk.

Only the upper ranks of actors have this kind of power, but it definitely is power and these actors are becoming less and less timid about wielding it. It's affected our thinking to the extent that one of the first mental exercises anyone does when reading a script is mentally casting the leads in the film. The first thought seems to be: "Who would be good for this film?" Fifty years ago, screenwriter Dudley Nichols had already made the observation that millions of people "will crowd the box offices if only those magic names are put up on the marquees, without regard for what sort of film it is."

Actors didn't climb onto the pedestal; they were put there by the movie executives, the chief engineers of the studio-machines who produce films. Nichols noted that actors reacted to their strength and position in one of two ways: "Some mistake their manufactured publicity for a special personal gift, for unique talent, and are the hardest to handle. The wiser accept it with a sigh and search for good screenplays and competent directors, knowing that only a personal standard will endure."

Bad or mediocre actors can do serious damage to a script. For example, when a famous (but humorless) actress read Neil Simon's script for *The Marrying Man*, she said, "Whoever wrote this [script] doesn't understand comedy." If anyone ever understood comedy, it was Neil Simon. The problem lies with the actor, in this case, not the writer.

Word has it that when *Hudson Hawk* won a Golden Raspberry Award for the worst script of the year in 1991, the co-writer, Steven de Souza had his assistant call the people who give the Razzies and tell them to send the award to Bruce Willis since he really deserved the screenwriting credit.

Sometimes the war between actors and writers gets dirty, as when Paul Rudnick, the author of the Broadway play, *I Hate Hamlet*, took a shot at his lead, Nicol Williamson. Rudnick complained in the *New York Times* that he rejected the adage that actors are either like cattle or children, because "Cattle can be legally slaughtered and children grow up."

The reverse can be true too. Good actors can save bad scripts. Jessica Lange told an interviewer for the *Los Angeles Times* "Calendar" section that, in *Cape Fear*, she and Nick Nolte "really made up a lot of our scenes. The roles really weren't there and I wouldn't have even considered doing the film if it wasn't for Marty [Scorsese], who wanted Nick and I to come up with our characters."

Lange makes it sound like Wesley Strick hadn't done his job as the writer. But that wasn't the case. "The thing about Jessica," responded Strick in an interview in *Hollywood Reporter*, "[is that] she made it clear that she signed on not because it was a brilliant character—which, by the way, it wasn't—but because she wanted to work with Marty and was told [the role] would be improved. When I wrote the script, I had no idea Jessica Lange was going to do it; it was basically just a generic character: the wife. She stands behind Nick a lot and whimpers."

Was Lange's complaint sour grapes? Or was Strick guilty of failing to develop his secondary characters? Either way, this example shows that actors can have a profound influence on a script.

An interesting sidebar: Gregory Peck and Robert Mitchum, both of whom starred in the original version of *Cape Fear* in 1962, read every line exactly as it was in James Webb's script. Neither actor felt the need to change a single word.

Some actors in their prime have started their own production companies and actively search for material to develop. With actors rising in power, you can see how they can enter the equation for choosing a screenwriter. If you can get a script to a bankable actor (someone whose name on the marquee is enough to generate millions of dollars), and that actor likes your script, then he or she may be the one to get your script off the ground, or, as everyone is fond of saying in the business, get your script green-lighted.

An Interview With Alan Arkin

I interviewed two very different actors for this book. The first actor I interviewed was Alan Arkin. He isn't what you'd call mainstream Hollywood. He's always been his own man, choosing a wide variety of roles, from comic to psychotic. He's had a remarkable career.

Alan Arkin started out in theater and worked his way to Second City where, with the likes of Mike Nichols and Elaine May, he learned the finely honed art of improvisation. Then he moved to film acting. His roles range from comic, sardonic and ironic in films like *The Russians Are Coming, the Russians Are Coming* (for which he won an Academy Award for Best Actor in 1966); *Catch 22*; *Edward Scissorhands*; and *Steal Big, Steal Little* to dramatic in films such as *The Heart Is a Lonely Hunter* (for which he was nominated for Best Actor); *Wait Until Dark*; *Havana*; and *Glengarry Glen Ross*.

Besides being an impressive actor, he's thoughtful and articulate, a deep-thinking man who's spent forty years understanding the nature of his craft.

Tobias: When you read a script, what *don't* you like to see in it?

Arkin: When writers think they have to explain everything about their characters, that turns me off. If a character starts making facial expressions, that turns me off. I feel the writer doesn't trust what he's put on the page and he's injecting my performance into the written word. If he does that, the first thing I do is stop reading. I don't want to see what my facial expressions are going to be. A common example in comedy would be, "He rolls his eyes toward heaven." If I see that in one more script. . . . You don't want to see things like that. You don't want to see what your facial expression is going to be or what your emotional reaction is going to be. If you have an understanding of your character in terms of his behavior and in terms of what he's saying, then you have to leave it with the actor to decide how that's going to be made visible on the screen.

Most actors are taught to throw out everything that's in parentheses in a script because we feel that's the writer saying, "Do you get it? Do you get it? Do you get what I'm telling you?" And if we don't get it, then you don't have any business writing the script in the first place.

Tobias: What if the writer wants a scene played in a way that isn't obvious? Do you like to see some personal direction then?

Arkin: Seeing words spread out through the script wouldn't have helped me in any way. For example, a few years ago Burt Reynolds asked my oldest son Adam to do a lead in a play at his theater in Florida. Adam asked me if I wanted to direct and since I love working with my family, I said, "Yeah, I'd love to direct it" even before I'd seen the script. And when Adam sent me the script, I didn't understand two consecutive words. I didn't have a clue what the play was about. I couldn't tell what the tone was—whether it was a comedy or tragedy or something between. And I consider myself a fairly astute reader.

So I said to Adam, "I'm committed to this, but I don't know what to do with it." He said, "I don't know what to do with it either." So I flew to Los Angeles and we sat around and just read it and read, Adam and I alone, and in a state—I started to panic because I still didn't have a clue what to do. We were reading the lines, we were reading the preface, we were reading between the lines, we were reading all the parentheses . . . nothing helped.

Then as a last resort, about three days into this, I said "Just for the hell of it, do it with an English accent."

Adam read the play with an English accent, and all of a sudden the whole thing became absolutely clear. It became clear what the writer had intended and what the play was about. And it also became clear that it was a comedy. Adam's English accent allowed us to see that the play was about people who had gigantic emotional lives and couldn't express them in any way. The English accent was the catalyst that unlocked the play for us. Only then could we drop the accent and find the emotional context that the play was written in.

I had to do the same thing with several of the other actors who said they'd do the play but didn't know what it was about either. I said, "Do it with an English accent," and bang, they all immediately understood the humor of the play.

Tobias: Was the play written by an Englishman?

Arkin: No. It was written by an American about Americans. But he was writing within a very, very specific emotional context that was nowhere in evidence. I think very often a writer's main message is something he's absolutely unaware of most of the time. A writer will say, "Yes, I'm doing a movie about the state of blah, blah, blah, and I want to do something about that." But what he's really doing is something completely removed from his stated purpose. He's got a subconscious text of his own that he's completely unaware of. It's one of the things that caused him to be a writer in the first place. There's a kind of subconscious necessity that a writer writes from that stays the same basically from project to project, and I don't think he's aware of the fact most of the time.

Tobias: Someone, I think it was Faulkner, made the observation that an author has only one book within him which he writes over and over.

Arkin: Right. One particular ax to grind. But if you're lucky and you're a person who's in a state of growth who's committed to your own personal growth rather than your growth as an artist—and I think there's a very distinct but important difference between those two things—then you have to change styles. You have to change styles in order to keep with who you are.

Tobias: Do you think it's possible for a screenwriter to maintain the same kind of artistic integrity as that of a novelist, for example?

Arkin: My son Tony just sold a treatment that's a murky, dark comedy. The studio he sold it to said, "It's not broad enough and it's not funny enough. We want it for a broader audience." He was in agony for a week, because he felt like he would be selling out, and that it would be a monstrous thing to do. And yet he had a murky, dark comedy he wanted to write. So he asked me what to do. And I said, "Well, just try it, so you know what you're leaving if you abandon this. Give it a shot. You're not going to lose your soul. See what it's like so that when you tell people for the next thirty years you hate it, you'll know what you're talking about. And if you're prone to sell out, then you'll find that out too. It's not going to change your basic sense of who you are by once attempting to do something that seems against the grain. Unless every cell in your body is screaming, "This is the wrong thing to do." There's a difference between that and feeling like your ego is being attacked.

So Tony worked, knocked himself out and came back with what is one of the funniest treatments I've ever read. He accomplished all of their needs and turned it into something witty and intelligent and stupid simultaneously.

It was a lesson for Tony too. You don't go through life without strictures put on you by others. As an actor I have strictures put on me all the time. It's a wonderful, but imaginary position to think you can sit at home and write something and that nobody's going to have any impact on it or influence or change it. If you think of the most pristine playwright in the world—anybody, Arthur Miller, Shakespeare, whoever—they didn't know what they had until they put it up in front of an audience. Even those so-called pure artists will change the way they view their own work. If an audience starts coughing half an hour into an Arthur Miller play, you bet he's going to start taking that seriously. Is that pandering? Is that changing? Or is that the recognition that theater and film are social forms that demand some kind of adjustment?

Tobias: Don't actors fall into the same trap as authors as far as giving the audience what it wants?

Arkin: I think most actors end up capitulating to what the system asks of them. They play the roles that everybody loved them in for so long and that they do so well. Stallone did that. He didn't even need to do it. He had enough money early on to make low-budget movies for the rest of his life and do any kind of thing he wanted and still be fabulously wealthy. But Stallone gave up after doing one really interesting project that got slammed called *Paradise Alley*.

Tobias: As an actor, how do you interpret a script character?

Arkin: I used to push myself as an actor. When a director would say to me, "I want you to play a scene this way," I would say, "No. I can't do it. I'm not going to do it that way. It's no good." The director would then ask why, and then I'd give him very lucid reasons why I didn't want to do it, why I *couldn't* do it, and that would be that.

But I've changed my approach in the past ten years. I will try things now that I wouldn't have used to try, to see if they work. I might say to the director, "I don't have a good feeling about it, but let's try it and see if I can make it work."

Very often it will work past any conception I had of how it would work. From that I now understand that a lot of my stance early on in my career came out of a rigidity and a kind of view of myself that limited what I was really capable of doing. You know, it comes out of fear.

Tobias: Fear that wouldn't allow you to take the risk?

Arkin: I'm more satisfied with who I am and therefore I can take risks that I wouldn't have taken before.

Tobias: Let's talk about *Catch 22*. Did Buck Henry write the role of Yossarian with Alan Arkin in mind?

Arkin: No. At that point nobody knew who I was. *I* didn't know who I was. I'd done nothing but character work up until that point. I'd never done anything that was remotely close to who I am as a person. I'd done *The Russians Are Coming, the Russians Are Coming, The Heart Is a Lonely Hunter* and *Wait Until Dark*. I mean who could tell who Alan Arkin was from those roles? As an actor my own intention was to hide as much as I possibly could, so I don't think Henry had any way of knowing how to write for me.

I asked Mike Nichols who Yossarian was, and he said, "He's you." That came as a shock to me because I didn't think anything was like me—including me. I was afraid at first that if I was just me on the screen there'd be a blank on the screen. You wouldn't see me at all because I didn't think I had any identity particularly. So it changed my career in a lot of ways. I'd go to the dailies and I'd say, "My God, there's actually somebody there." I didn't know who it was, but I could see there was somebody on the screen. So it gave me a sense that it was me all along that was doing things to myself rather than it being something that I was inventing from whole cloth, a character.

Tobias: What would you say to the writer who claims to have written the perfect role for Alan Arkin?

Arkin: I probably wouldn't want to read it, because that would mean they'd put me into a pigeonhole, and I don't want to play that part because I played it already. I'm not a businessman. I'm not in it to open a store, to have an aspirin bottle with a label on it. A lot of actors are acting because success is more important to them than any kind of journey of self-discovery either as a person or an artist—if I can even use that term in film anymore. But for a writer to tell me he's got the perfect role for me, that bores me to death. I don't want to do that. If I did it already, it's an inducement for me not to do it again.

Tobias: Is that a realization you came to later in life or have you known it all along?

Arkin: I felt it from the beginning. In fact, I'm starting to soften on it. I have to soften it periodically when it comes time to earn a living.

Tobias: Looking back, you went from a Russian sailor in *The Russians Are Coming, the Russians Are Coming*, to a deaf mute in *The Heart Is a Lonely Hunter*, to a psychotic killer in *Wait Until Dark*. It would've been hard to say, "I'm going to write a role for Alan Arkin."

Arkin: That hurt my career. I kept getting wonderful feedback from people and reviews, but I didn't get work consistently. That was because I wasn't someone you thought of first in a role because nobody knew what I did. And then after they ran through the people they knew could play the part—because they'd played it before already—then somebody would say, "What about Alan Arkin?" and somebody would say, "Hey, that's an interesting idea."

Tobias: But it kept you from being typecast.

Arkin: Which I liked. But what was interesting is that most of my works for a long while were as an outsider, somebody from a completely different civilization, a stranger in a strange land. That was certainly true of *The Russians Are Coming*, it was true of *Poppy*, it was true of *The Heart Is a Lonely Hunter*, and it was true of *Wait Until Dark*. It was even true of *Catch 22*. A fish out of water. It was true of the plays I'd done on Broadway before that too. It was true of most of the things I decided to do in Second City before that, and that was all stuff I'd inflicted upon myself. There's a subconscious message I'm giving an audience. I guess

producers and writers were picking up on that, so I was offered parts
that may have seemed very, very varied on the surface that had the
underpinning of somebody who's a stranger in a strange land.

Tobias: How do you reconcile Alan Arkin the person with Alan Arkin
the actor in a role?

Arkin: As an actor I'm given tremendous freedom. The last film I did
was directed by Andrew Davis, (*Under Siege, The Fugitive*) who just had
two gigantic hits and is sought after by every studio in the world for an
enormous sum of money, and I had *carte blanche*. I changed every line
in the thing. I was given an opportunity to improvise continuously. And
I get spoiled by that. I feel like people come to me a lot of times because
they know I come out of an improvisation theater (Second City), and
I'm changing the dialogue significantly at least two-thirds of the time.
I'm changing the direction of a character. I'm reshaping. And I come
in almost on a daily basis with new ideas, new sketches for scenes. It's
not because I feel like I have to or because I feel like I have an agenda.
I just feel like things are sloppy and not really well thought out.

Tobias: In terms of the writer's depiction of character?

Arkin: Yes. I can understand why to a certain extent, because there are
so many hands in the pie now. There's so many people with so many
agendas that writers by and large don't want to reveal that much of
themselves or put their pain or joys on the page because it's just going
to get trampled on. So you say, "What do you want to put yourself on
the line for? It's going to get changed anyway."

Tobias: So the days of Paddy Chayefsky scripts are gone?

Arkin: Pretty much. There's some work coming out of England now
that has wonderful language in it. Anything that Anthony Hopkins does
has a wonderful sense of language. And there are things from the Latin
American countries that have a wonderful sense of language.

Tobias: Since you came out of such a strong improvisation background,
do you feel that when a character is given to you that it's up to you to
shape it, fulfill it? Or do you think that's just what actors do?

Arkin: That's what actors do. One thing that's unique in improvisational
actors that I've found is that when I hire an improvisational actor I
find that he almost invariably and instinctively knows right from the
beginning what function his character has in the whole. A lot of times
actors will read their parts and not pay attention to what's going on
around—you know, they won't read the entire script. I think musicians
do that too. The oboe player will read the oboe part. He wouldn't read
the entire score to see what function the oboe plays in the entity of the

piece. And it's a shame, because if any actor gets a sense of what the play is first, he gets an intuitive sense of what he must do. There are very few actors who work that way.

Tobias: It sounds like you're saying that an actor is an enabler of character. That it's not simply putting on a suit of clothes that the writer has provided. It's taking a concept that the writer has provided and then enabling it.

Arkin: Exactly. If you're lucky, maybe once or twice in your life a writer will come to you and say, "God, you got things out of the character I didn't know I'd put on the paper."

Tobias: What do you miss most in scripts right now? The literature, the poetry, the soul. . . .

Arkin: Not that I speak that beautifully, but I miss language among people that are capable of doing it. Language gives something to rest on when you're an actor. It's like having a foundation, a floor that's solid beneath you. Very few scripts I read anymore have a specific stamp of a writer on them, either in terms of language or the rhythm of the scene, which is another language. The wording has a rhythm, and then a sense of scene structure will also have a certain rhythm, and very often that will let you know who a writer is.

Tobias: Like David Mamet?

Arkin: Read half a page of Mamet and you know who you're dealing with. That was the hardest thing I've ever worked on in my life because of the exactitude of his wording. We rehearsed for a month, and even with rehearsal all the time, Ed Harris and I used to go in the trailer and run and run the scenes and run them and run them and run them. I've never worked so hard on anything in my life, including Shakespeare. If I had a line that was, "I'm sorry, I, I, I," the script supervisor would stop me and say, "Alan, you only said three 'I's."

Tobias: Your role in *Glengarry Glen Ross* had more feeling and thought to it than the others. Was that the way it was written in the script?

Arkin: My initial reaction when they offered me the part was, "Ah, yeah, they gave me the *in-laws'* character." They gave me the jerk. The nice guy who's the jerk. And I said, "I don't want to play this part." Then half a dozen people convinced me I should do it. So I said, "OK, if I play this part, I get to transform it so he's not *that* guy. I want to find something else about him that I can feel good about. I want to feel good about this guy in some way."

I had a feeling that Mamet knew my character had to be in the piece, but I don't think he was comfortable writing about him. So he turned him into a schmuck. But I didn't want to play him that way. I gave my character a subtext which is that he's not a salesman. I said, "He's not a salesman. He's a grammar school teacher. He's been a grammar school teacher for twenty years and got fired from the school because they were cutting back on teachers and he didn't have tenure. And he couldn't get a job as anything else, so he's now in this job he hates." Instead of making him incompetent, as Mamet had him, I made him somebody who just didn't know that work.

Tobias: A stranger in a strange land?

Arkin: Yes, but it gave him dignity. My character has the only line in the script that has any sense of moral responsibility to it. It's only one line, but I think it's very telling. Ed Harris is talking to me about how it's bad business to do a certain thing in a certain way, and I say, "Yeah, bad for the customers." It's only one line, but it tells us how he's thinking. In some way he wants to serve something, unlike anybody else in the piece.

Tobias: Then do you see a script as a blueprint or do you see it as something from which you take those plans and build your own sense of character?

Arkin: It depends on the script. If I'm reading a Mamet script, then it's infinitely more like a blueprint. It's something I have to live up to as an actor because it's got integrity and it's got a voice and it's got a statement. And as such I feel I have to find my way into his idea of what life is. I have to become part of Mamet's philosophy, his rhythm. Rhythm is philosophy, whether you like it or not.

Tobias: You're talking about the writer's strength of presence.

Arkin: Exactly. I have no problem at all doing that with a piece if I can feel that kind of integrity in it. I love doing that. But then it depends on the director to make sure everybody's in that same ballpark. It can become very complicated. I have to have long talks now with the director before I do anything. If it's a piece with enormous integrity, like Mamet's work, I want to find out what their needs are and see if I feel like I can fit into those parameters.

If it's a piece that *doesn't* have a lot of integrity but I feel I can make something out of the character, then I want to tell the director what I want to do with it and see if he's going to live with that. Or at least find out how he's going to make the film, how he's going to give it integrity that I'm not seeing on the printed page. Either way I'm comfortable working as long as there's some sense of philosophy at work.

Tobias: So you're saying that in the absence of a philosophy of character, you'll create one?

Arkin: If I can find something in the character that I feel can give some integrity to it.

Tobias: Do most scripts fail to create that kind of depth for their characters?

Arkin: Ninety-nine percent of the time, even in good scripts. You rarely find anything with the kind of integrity that Mamet has.

Tobias: Anyone else?

Arkin: Robert Downey. Not the actor, but his father, the writer-director (*Putney Swope, Greaser's Palace*). When you read a Downey script you know it's Robert Downey. Nobody thinks like him and nobody writes like him. Nobody's got his rhythm. For years I wanted to work with him because I admired his early films. They're completely nuts and completely individual.

Tobias: Do you think anyone is writing good scripts anymore?

Arkin: I'm having trouble with American movies these days. Every movie I see is technically perfect but doesn't have any blood or heart in it. I don't remember anything I see anymore. I can't remember sixteen frames of any American film I see. I thought I was getting Alzheimer's disease. I thought there was something seriously wrong with me. Until I saw some little tiny film by Satyajit Ray that he made twenty-five years ago and I could remember every frame of it. While I was watching it, I said, "This is boring. It's so simplistic." And then by the end of the film I was sobbing my eyes out, and I could remember every frame of it.

Tobias: Do you remember the name of the film?

Arkin: It's called *The Post Office*. It's wonderful. A heartbreaking, wrenching, beautiful, simple piece. Ray does more with a suggestion than American directors and writers can do with $100,000 worth of explosions.

Tobias: Do you think that's because American society is largely comfortable and it's got nothing to motivate it anymore. It's secure, it's warm, it's cozy.

Arkin: I wouldn't say comfortable. I'd say sated. We need more and more stimulation in order to feel like we're feeling anything. Subtlety is gone. I think ambiguity is gone. There's no such thing as a film that doesn't define itself as either a comedy or a drama or a tragedy. I can't think of an American film that crosses those lines anymore.

If I do a lecture at a school, everybody says, "What's wrong with

Hollywood? Why are they going . . ." I said, "Wait. You don't understand. If you were paying to see Bible stories, they would make Bible stories twenty-four hours a day for you." The reason they're not getting Bible stories with wonderful morals and nice sunsets and beautiful language is because no one's going to see them. I said, "That doesn't mean that studios are moral. They're less moral than even you think they are, but they don't care. They have no agenda other than making money.

Tobias: And if we decide suddenly we want good, artistic pictures, that's what we're going to get?

Arkin: They'd be happy to do that. They don't care any more about those than they do about the ones they're making now. Did you see blah, blah, blah? The whole bottom line is that a movie made a half a billion dollars. That's its value. That's all I hear about. I don't hear about values or the view of a changing society. That's what art used to do. It used to have a great moral purpose. It doesn't anymore. It's to take our minds off our lives and to bring in the bucks.

Tobias: What advice do you have for screenwriters, outside of the. . . .

Arkin: Don't do it.

Tobias: Don't do it?

Arkin: Don't do it unless you have to. Don't write for a studio. Don't tailor make your stuff for other people. Get another job and write on spec.

Tobias: Write the script that's inside you?

Arkin: And write them small enough so there's a bigger possibility of getting them done. Do what John Patrick Shanley did. He wrote *Moonstruck* and then auditioned directors himself. They didn't tell him what they wanted. He told them what he wanted. I think that's the way to do it unless you end up feeling that you're not talented enough to do that. And if you want to be a screenwriter bad enough, then I guess you gotta just start bending.

Tobias: I know a Director of Photography who was reading a script for television that began with the line, "Mr. Green was walking down the street with five thousand years of Jewish suffering on his face." The DP said, "That's not filmable. How do you show five thousand years of Jewish suffering on somebody's face?" But the producer of the show loved the line so much that he bought the script. Do you like to see that kind of writing in a script, where the writer isn't writing a movie, but writing a piece of literature?

Arkin: That doesn't bother me as long as the next line tells me something else. As long as the first line out of his mouth is a deflection off of what that statement is. A man walks down the street and he's got five thousand years of Jewish pain and suffering on his face. The first line out of his mouth is, "Oh, God, I can't live another day like this." I know I'm in trouble already. If the first line out of his mouth is he's on the phone to his nineteen-year-old girlfriend, then I say, "Wait a minute. There's a guy who's got some sense of irony, some sense of contrast." Then I want to know what the third line is going to be.

A movie is a game you play that gives you a philosophy. It's a hypothesis. Everybody writing a book, writing a piece of music, or writing a movie is giving a lesson in philosophy. The first ten minutes is the hypothesis, and then the rest of the movie is conclusion. This is what human life is like, and this is what people are like. The hypothesis is only interesting if you show the angles of it. You've got to see the idea being deflected off a lot of different walls. If it's only one statement that's repeated over and over, then the statement has no way of being challenged. The idea has got to be bounced off a lot of different contexts in order to really hold water. The more context, the more walls it bounces off of, the more exciting it is, and the more chance you have of really thinking that the conclusion amounts to something.

Tobias: So a philosophy shouldn't just be stated but proven too?

Arkin: You can't just say, "This is what life should be." That's terribly dangerous for a writer. Art shouldn't be polemic, but experience. It's got to be your experience. It's got to be the welding between your beliefs and your experience. The writer shouldn't be a politician.

But nobody wants to admit to any kind of philosophy anymore. Art started out as either a joyful expression of a relationship with God or a desire to give people that sense. Now it's just entertainment. I don't like entertainment. It doesn't have a lot of value.

Tobias: Chekhov wrote that real art rests upon what he called "the dunghill." That was his way of saying that ninety-nine percent of all so-called art is really junk. But it is precisely junk that gives art its value. That's how we recognize real art, by its apartness, its distinctness from the junk that's being produced in volume. Do you think you're being too severe by saying that all films should live up to the standards of high art?

Arkin: One problem is that nobody's encouraged to do anything of value. There's no sense there's anything for you if you write something of value. There's no reward at the end of the road.

Tobias: Does there need to be a reward? Recognition by an audience or. . . .

Arkin: Being able to continue to work, I suppose. That's what every writer wants, isn't it?

An Interview With Charlton Heston

Charlton Heston represents all the grand traditions of Hollywood. The range of characters in this man's genealogy is as broad as literature itself: Michelangelo, Ben-Hur, El Cid, Moses, Antony (of *Antony and Cleopatra*), to name a few. He's worked with such directoral giants as Cecil B. DeMille, William Wyler and Orson Welles. Talking to him gives the impression that he carries within him a half-century of American filmmaking. And if Alan Arkin is typical of the Hollywood outsider, then Charlton Heston is typical of the Hollywood insider.

Tobias: What attracts an actor to a script?

Heston: Like every actor, I'm interested in how good the part is. Suppose it's some marvelous madcap comedy in which I play a nutty admiral. I'm really not going to be interested in a role like that. Then I ask myself, "Does this have a chance of being a good picture?" No script in the history of movies ever had more than an outside chance of being a good picture because it depends upon all kinds of factors that you can't determine from the script.

Tobias: Are you talking about the politics of making a film?

Heston: If you want to call it that. There's an unpredictable mix of producer, director and actors on the set. You can't accurately foresee what's going to happen to a script during its journey from the script to the screen. These are things the screenwriter can't control or even plan for. There's a history of great scripts that never got produced in Hollywood.

So if I'm interested in a script, then I want to know who else is involved. Who's producing, who's directing, who the other actors are. That will give me a better idea of what chance the film has of becoming a good film.

If I like the part and they're making an appropriate (financial) offer, then I may accept the role.

Tobias: How important is the money in relation to the script?

Heston: The key word is appropriate. Sometimes they may make me a minimal offer. I've done Shakespearean films for a quarter of the money that I command in the market. Everyone understands that. There are parts on high-quality but low-budget, low-prospect films that you just say yes to because the parts are so good. You can easily get actors for these kinds of parts. Actors are by and large quite generous, even A-list actors.

Tobias: Once you've accepted a role, then what do you do?

Heston: I ask myself, "What should be better about it?" Depending on the kind of clout you have [as an actor], then you have a chance to make some changes. For a long time I've been able to do that. Unfortunately for the writer, the problem with working at the very top level is that the project is essentially taken out of the writer's hands. That's going to happen in any event.

Tobias: What's the most useful thing you could say to a screenwriter?

Heston: In theater the play is the thing. It's the writer's medium, whereas film is the director's medium. In theater you get good actors and a good director and good scene designers and you put on the play. And if the actors are right and the play's any good and the sets are not terrible, it'll work. But a screenplay isn't the written version of the movie. This is the hardest thing for a screenwriter to accept.

A screenplay is, at best, the architectural plan of a movie that will be altered, as it must be, by the input of the director and the leading actor, the editor and, to a lesser degree, the cinematographer. A play is words, and you have an actor to speak the words and someone to tell the actors where to stand, and get some light on them. But a screenplay is an *idea*. Because a movie is pictures, and you find again and again that the less you say and more you show, the better you are. It's simply impossible to write that. You discover that. And it's a very hard concept for screenwriters to accept.

Tobias: To get into visualization of character?

Heston: You can't write visualization. You discover it when you're on the set in Kenya or Mozambique or in Montana. You'll suddenly discover something that says the whole thing. That's happened to me many times on movies.

And many different kinds of people have become significant directors. Designers like Alfred Hitchcock, cinematographers like George Stevens and David Lean, assistant directors like William Wyler and Jack Forbes. I can think of only one writer—Billy Wilder—who became an important director.

Tobias: Why do you think that is?

Heston: I don't know, but it's true. I know there are writers who become directors. John Milius, for example. But one suspects that perhaps their primary instinct in the beginning was as a director.

Tobias: If I understand you correctly you're saying that a screenplay is a template, and a film is always in the process of becoming?

Heston: That's right. Studio heads always want to say, "OK. Now this is the shooting draft. The final draft. We're going to put 'final draft' on this version." You may have had two or three revisions, maybe with a couple different screenwriters. And everybody says, "Yeah, OK, that's good." And then they say, "All right. Final draft." And they think by putting that on the cover it means it's not going to be changed. That's ridiculous. Of course it's going to be changed. Even if the whole film takes place in an interior in Hollywood, it's going to be changed. The picture, by which I mean the frame—the undiscovered frame—is what you're after.

Tobias: The undiscovered frame?

Heston: I never read the script of *All Quiet on the Western Front* [written by Lewis Milestone, Maxwell Anderson, Del Andrews and George Abbott—author's note], but I know that it's probably true that the last sequence with Lew Ayres aiming for the butterfly on the wall of the trench and then you hear the off-screen rifle shot . . . you can't write that. You've got to discover it.

Tobias: Do you think the screenwriter should be included on the set or do you think he or she should be kept out of the production process?

Heston: I've done films where the writer has stayed on during the shoot or new writers have been called in. Sometimes they do it without salary, sometimes with. Personally I think it's a good idea, but once the camera starts to turn, the screenwriter ceases to be the central creative element. That's hard for most writers to accept. They tend to take a proprietary interest in their work, which runs against the grain of the process of filmmaking.

Tobias: Do you see any fundamental change in the way scripts are being written now as opposed to forty years ago?

Heston: There's more sex and violence, but then there's been sex and violence in the dramas since the Greeks and Elizabethans. The problem today with sex and violence graphically displayed on the screen is that it loses its impact after awhile. The more graphically you display it, the less effective it is, especially with sex, because, except for the partici-pants, sex is visually pretty funny to look at. I mean, humping along above somebody. You've got to find another way to shoot it. The graphic display of the physical organs of sex isn't terribly exciting unless you're into that sort of thing. Indeed, it's pretty funny.

Chapter Six

Inside the Producer

A script can begin its life anywhere after it's written: with an agent, a producer, a director or even an actor if he or she has a production company or enough box-office clout to make someone else (such as an agent, producer or director) listen. While most scripts come up through authorized channels (e.g., through an agent) other scripts make headway by coming in through the back or side door. When Robert Redford was making *Ordinary People* in 1980, John Baily, his cinematographer, passed a copy of *The Milagro Beanfield War* by John Nichols to Redford and suggested he read it. Redford did read the book and, eight years later, made the film. Such stories are not uncommon.

By far, however, the gateway for most scripts is through the producer. There are two basic types of producers. The *executive producer* is usually the person who puts together the financial package that makes a film possible. He (or she) is responsible for the legal and financial structure of the film and may occasionally get involved in the creative life of the film itself. The executive producer is a businessperson. You need no credentials to be a deal maker. If you can find money to make a film, then, in effect, you're an executive producer. The *producer*, on the other hand, functions as the head of a film on a practical, day-to-day basis and provides the network of support for the director's artistic vision, while coordinating all phases of production. In the public's eye, the director may seem like the boss, and in terms of the agreed upon vision of the film, she is; but the producer is the overseer, and if he doesn't like what the director is doing, he may have the right and power to change directors. Depending on the film's structure, the producer may be the ultimate authority.

Now that the studio system has given way to independents, the power that traditionally was the sole domain of studio heads is shared with independent producers.

The independent producer usually has his or her own staff and develops deals with either the major studios (Paramount, Warner Brothers, Twentieth Century Fox, Disney, etc.) or with leading independent production companies such as Miramax, Tri-Star, etc. The independent producer usually develops the property (script) and oversees its production. To develop a property means to find it, arrange financing, establish a legal identity for the production, and put together key personnel, called the above-the-line production staff, which typically includes the director, the writer and cast. These decisions are made in concert with the director.

An independent producer may also sign a multi-picture deal with a studio. (For example, a producer might contract to develop and produce six films in a ten-year period for a studio.) A producer at the top of his or her form may have as many as a dozen different projects in various stages of development at any given time. That means they always have an eye out for new properties.

Producers who contract to provide films for a studio (or a large independent distributor) take huge (and sometimes personal) financial risks when they make a big budget film of $50 million or more. While the possibility of a $200- to $500-million return is always alluring to a studio, very few films make that kind of money. It's more common for big budget films to "tank," meaning an investment of $50 million only returns $4 million. Translation: Some producers tend to favor smaller budget films (under $8 million). A small (or smaller) budget film may be easier to sell and carries less risk. A decently made film in this category is fairly certain to make back its investment with foreign and domestic sales and video rental income. While these films are rarely blockbusters, they are conservative hedges to the big money gambles. The beginning screenwriter is wise to consider this fact.

Successful producers have three important skills. First, they have experience. They've been around, know the ropes, have done at least one notable film of either critical or financial success. Second, they have contacts. They know people. They can call the head of a studio or an agency or an actor and *get the call returned*. And lastly, they know people with money willing to invest in the right stuff.

An Interview With Patrick Markey

Patrick Markey is an independent producer. He was a producer on *The Joy Luck Club*, *A River Runs Through It* (with Robert Redford), *The Quick and the Dead* (directed by Sam Raimi) and *Bogus* (directed by

Norman Jewison), among others.

   Patrick is a maverick. He's very particular about the kinds of stories he pursues. His films don't always play to the stands: *The Joy Luck Club* and *A River Runs Through It* are good examples. Patrick seeks stories about people. He develops projects that other producers may disregard because they might be perceived as too pensive. In his words, "I prefer stories about the love, understanding and misunderstanding within families. These emotional experiences are universal to all of us."

Tobias: What are the most common faults you find in scripts these days?

Markey: My chief complaint is that the majority of scripts submitted to me are repetitive. Too many writers rework ideas that have become trite as opposed to coming up with something that's really original. Most screenplays are formulaic. That's why I'm drawn to novels. Novelists generally create original ideas, ideas that haven't been explored yet. Rarely do I get a screenplay that is fresh and original.

Tobias: In your mind, what is more important, plot or character?

Markey: I'm interested in stories that emanate from character as opposed to a plot that has characters attached to it. For the last ten years in Hollywood there's been an unfortunate emphasis on the conceptual idea of a movie—a one-sentence pitch that characterizes the film. I much prefer starting with character. Character evolves from a story that we can put on a linear track and develop a three-act structure around. Ultimately it becomes more resonant and significant to the viewer than something that's strictly a conceptual piece, a story that's easy to pitch but doesn't ask anything of its audience.

Tobias: Do you think there's much of a future in films like *The Joy Luck Club* and *A River Runs Through It.*

Markey: Pieces like those are literary and not easy sells. They're not high concept pictures. They're intimate stories, and yet both movies had very respectful showings at the box office. It is our primary responsibility as producers to make movies people want to see. They can't be precious film festival fair that a hundred people go see. That kind of film doesn't reach out and attract an audience on a wide scale. It's our job as producers to find material that speaks to us as artists, but a successful film must pay for itself.

Tobias: How important is dialogue?

Markey: Dialogue is foremost. It defines character. But it all must work within a structure.

Tobias: If you could talk directly to the writer, what kind of advice would you give?

Markey: I believe it was Kurt Luedke (*Absence of Malice, Out of Africa*) who said that almost anyone can write a screenplay, but almost no one can write one well. I would urge any first-time screenwriter to seriously ponder that thought. Writing a screenplay appears to be pretty straight-forward. I'd counsel anyone who is going to write a screenplay not to go at it with the arrogance that it is easy. "Oh, I saw a movie last week, I can better than that." It's a lot harder process than people think. But if you feel you have a story to tell, an idea that you can express best in a screenplay, then sit down and do it. But don't write it because you expect to make a million dollars. Write it because you have to write it. Write it because your muse is telling you this is what you need to do. Then the ideas will be honest and believeable.

Tobias: Any other advice?

Markey: Yes, write scenes that capture the imagination of the reader first. Your script has to reach out and attract a producer, a director and eventually actors. But don't be original just for the sake of being original, because your story won't touch anyone. A film should appeal to its view-ers. It should have some sort of universality to it without being a cliché. Your script should should explore the larger questions that we're faced with as human beings. Figure out some way your story can reach people who are struggling their way through this world.

Tobias: What's the best way to approach a producer with an idea?

Markey: Do your homework. If someone wants to bring a script to me, they should know that my work primarily deals with family relation-ships. I'm very interested in the complicated dynamics within families, and our longing to better understand those we love as we get into our middle years. It's true of *River* and *Joy Luck* and with the picture I'm doing now (*The Tie That Binds*). I keep going back to those themes, revisiting that territory. It has a lot of appeal to me, and I've been able to find in each of those pieces the sort of narrative thread that compels me as an artist and directs me to commit a year of my life working diligently to get it produced. If you do your homework, you'll know what kind of picture appeals to which producer. That's half the battle.

Tobias: Do you agree with the principle that writers ought to target scripts to producers?

Markey: Don't target anybody. Write what you feel, and write what you know. If it's good, then I'll respond to it. Don't strive to write a screenplay that's going to please Patrick Markey. Write a screenplay that answers a need in your soul, and if you've been honest with yourself, there's a much better chance that they will have something that I'd be interested in looking at. Don't waste your time trying to figure out something to write that's going to get my attention. After *A River Runs Through It*, all the fly-fishing scripts came my way. I don't want to do another fly-fishing movie, I already did that. I want to go on to other territory. If you write with honesty and integrity, then there's a good chance that it would appeal to me.

Tobias: What about practical considerations in scriptwriting such as writing for a particular star or being careful not to write two lead competing roles?

Markey: That's gimmick writing. Don't write something for Meryl Streep, don't write something for Bruce Willis. Write the piece, if it's well written, then the actors will respond to it. Serious actors are *desperate* for well-written material. There's so little of it. If you write something well and from the heart, you can get good actors to do it. They'll fight for your work to get produced.

Tobias: What about writing action films?

Markey: God knows there are writers in town who have that formulaic thing down and can crank out those two-million-dollar, action-dominated screenplays. But I don't produce those kind of movies, so I'm not the guy to talk to.

Tobias: How important is it to you for a writer to follow closely standard script format?

Markey: If a script is loose, it's fine. Don't feel a need to meticulously follow the format. I care more about the structure of the story. We all know that a three-act structure is an extremely important element of the screenplay based upon the way a movie works. My training is in theatre, so I'm more inclined to look at a piece of drama in terms of its act structure. But the format is much less of a concern for me than the ideas. If you have a well reasoned, articulate piece, I can find any number of typists in town to put the script into proper format.

Tobias: How do you feel about writers who include camera direction in their scripts?

Markey: The screenplays I like best have minimal stage directions and camera angles. The director and the cameraperson do that, not the writer. I don't need a writer to tell me where to put the camera. I need him to set up the idea, and we'll figure out the rest. Too may screenplays are cleverly designed, but there's nothing inside that design. A beautiful frame with no picture in it, form without content.

Tobias: Do you feel that many writers would rather be directors than writers?

Markey: Exactly. I don't need the writer to tell me what he knows about directing or cinematography. I want to read what the writer knows about writing character and dialogue.

Tobias: Story, story, story?

Markey: Always, back to character and emotion and what's going on in these people's lives.

Tobias: What level of descriptive detail do you like to see in a script?

Markey: I like detail in the novelistic sense. I like to get an atmospheric sense of place and time and character, but I don't need an abundance of the technical details and elements of filmmaking. That's my job. Screenplays that are written minimally are much more appealing to me because they're written more like poetry. Keep details relevant. I don't need to know the model number and color of the Corvette in the scene. I can figure that out if you give me the characters.

Tobias: Can you give us an example of that kind of writer?

Markey: Early in my career I was involved with *Ordinary People*. Alvin Sargent wrote the screenplay. He's not prolific, he doesn't crank them out, but he writes so beautifully and capably. There's little stage direction and minimal editorializing about how to make the movie. It's seamlessly written, and from that, ideas abound about how to make it into a picture. He writes with such discipline; his pared-down style is like reading poetry. Richard Friedenberg (*A River Runs Through It*) writes the same way. He has a very lean style that doesn't get overly complicated with camera direction. It's about the story that's on the page. That's what I prefer from a screenwriter.

I also admire Becky Johnson's work, as well as Richard LaGravanese, Steve Zallian and Nora Ephron. William Goldman's screenplays are wonderful (*Butch Cassidy and the Sundance Kid*, *The Princess Bride*). Paddy Chayefsky (*Hospital*, *Network*) was a great writer who also wrote for television in its prouder days. He had a brilliant sense of social and political commentary. Anything he put his pen to had resonance.

Tobias: Since you seem to like films that derive from novels, could you tell us the differences between the two?

Markey: *The Joy Luck Club* is a good example of how a popular novel translates to film. The novel is extremely wide ranging. It crosses several generations and contains something like thirty different stories cutting back and forth. Amy Tan's book is beautiful, heartbreaking. Amy had never written a screenplay before so Wayne teamed her up with Ron

Bass to write the adaptation. Ron Bass is one of the most experienced screenwriters in Hollywood, and he helped give the screenplay structure by creating that family party that runs throughout the film. We start and end with the party, and we return to it over and over and let the different stories emanate from there. The novel didn't have that device—it didn't need it—but the film did.

Tobias: How can a beginning writer break in?

Markey: I believe that if you write a good story then it will find its way. I don't really think there are many great undiscovered scripts lying around unproduced. The network for finding scripts has expanded over the last fifteen or twenty years and if people have good ideas, those scripts will be pursued.

I just produced a movie for television written by a woman in North Dakota. She had been a teacher and had never written a script. I don't believe she had ever even been outside of North Dakota. When she finished her script, she sent it to a company in Ohio that encourages and develops regional writers and they sent it to me. I saw that it wasn't a feature, but that it had potential as a TV movie. I sent it to a production company and they sent it to Ann Margaret. She liked it, and now it has been produced.

There are a lot of people who know a good script when they read it. Regional film schools are a great source. People who teach screenwriting, that kind of thing.

Tobias: Should a writer pay attention to what it costs to produce a scene?

Markey: A writer should just write it. I'm currently developing a project that takes place in a Japanese internment camp during World War II. It's set in Wyoming in the early 1940s. It will be expensive to produce. It has battle scenes in the South Pacific, then cuts to war-ready San Diego with armed troopships in port. That film could cost $75 million. But there are a dozen other ways I could approach the material to economize. I have the ability as a producer—especially with my experience as a line producer—to look at the story and figure out ways of paring it down without compromising the piece. The writer has to rely on us to do that. If they primarily write to a budget the story isn't going to be as good. Write the piece fully, flesh it out and don't hold back. If you require Armageddon in your screenplay, write Armageddon: I'll figure out how to produce it.

▪ Chapter Seven ▪

Inside the Director of Photography

The Director of Photography—known simply as the DP—is responsible for the visual look of the film. He seldom operates the camera himself, but rather supervises other people who run the cameras. The DP works directly with the director and others to achieve a sense of the visual style and content of the script as it goes through the process of transforming the word into image. As the head cinematographer, the DP is also responsible for the lighting and the technical elements involved in setting up shots.

The DP is a key position. He's involved in the interpretive process from the beginning, even before a camera is brought to the set. The DP consults with the director about the film's look, but good directors usually rely on the creative talents of good DPs to interpret that need. The director hardly has time to visualize every detail of a shot, scene or sequence in a film, so he or she must rely on the expertise and creative talents of the DP.

Worldwide there are probably less than a thousand DPs in the top line, feature film business. They're a very small, select group of people. A producer or a director decides upon a DP whom he knows from previous experiences. Each DP has his or her own cachet or style, and the producer and director choose accordingly.

Once chosen, the DP reads your script and then makes critical judgments about every scene in the screenplay. As a result, the DP makes a major creative contribution to the look and feel of your film. As the screenwriter, you should speak to the DPs needs in order to convey the visual sense of what your story is about. If this isn't important to you, then don't worry about it, but if you see your film inside your head a certain way, then you should write your screenplay in such a way that it conveys those visual ideas to the DP. Probably the single most important thing you can do, however, is to keep your description to a minimum.

The temptation to describe is great in any writer, but in film, less is better. You'll notice that *without exception*, every person interviewed for this book prefers simple, descriptive strokes rather than elaborate detail.

An Interview With Andrew Laszlo

Andy Laszlo has been a Director of Photography for fifty years. After apprenticing in Europe, he arrived in the United States as a refugee from Europe in 1947 with $2.63 in his pocket. He couldn't speak any English. Since that time, and through what he calls persistence and good luck, he worked his way up the ranks and became a DP for such television shows as *You'll Never Get Rich*, *Naked City*, *Coronet Blue*, *I Remember Mama* and many other shows. He worked on the *Ed Sullivan Show* and his television experience culminated with the epic mini-series *Shogun*, based on James Clavell's novel.

In 1964 Andy shot his first feature film, *One Potato, Two Potato*. Since then, he's DP-ed over forty films including *You're a Big Boy Now* (1967), *The Night They Raided Minsky's* (1968), *The Out-of-Towners* (1970), the cult favorite *The Warriors* (1979), *Rambo: First Blood* (1982), *Streets of Fire* (1984), *Innerspace* (1987) and *Star Trek V: The Final Frontier* (1989). He's worked with the likes of Francis Ford Coppola, Stephen Spielberg and Walter Hill. Among cinematographers, Andy Laszlo is a dean.

Tobias: How do you reconcile the creative vision of the writer with the creative vision of the cinematographer?

Laszlo: At times it's very difficult; it's almost impossible to balance the two. The screenwriter commits his ideas to the page on the basis of his imagination or historical research, as in the case of James Clavell's *Shogun*. I interpret the writer's ideas—they're the basis for everything I have to pay close attention to—but at the same time I have to contribute my own ideas. Yes, I have to interpret the written page, but I also have to interpret the director's and the producer's ideas. It's not like a painter who can take a canvas and paint anything he wants.

Tobias: Do you like the writer to give you a lot of detail?

Laszlo: Some writers make the mistake of trying to be too vivid or trying to give extremely detailed descriptions of everything in their script.

Tobias: Give an example of how a DP visually interprets script detail.

Laszlo: I was working on a picture called *First Blood*. In it there's a shot of Sylvester Stallone entering a police station that he just shot up at night. The script calls for Rambo to shoot out all the lights in town, but I knew that wasn't practical—he would've had to shoot out a thousand lights. Instead, I suggested that he shoot out the transformers so whole sections of the town would go dark. This was a practical solution to a script problem, but it also affected the photography, the look of the film—in other words, the visual interpretation of the script. It's the middle of the night and there isn't a speck of light. In reality the town would've been totally dark. But I couldn't just put a blank, dark screen up there. I had to consider the writer's intent and create an illusion of darkness that is visually pleasing and still serves the story.

Part of *First Blood* takes place in an abandoned mine that Rambo gets trapped in. The script called for Rambo to find his way out of the mine and cave. He accomplishes this by fashioning a torch from strips of his shirt soaked in kerosene that he finds in the rubble of the mine. Being the highly trained, ingenious Green Beret, Rambo notices the flames of his torch being bent by a draft of air in the cave. He follows this draft to a mine shaft, a way out of the cave. Creating the telltale draft was expertly accomplished by our special effects crew, who, by the use of fans and other air moving equipment could make the flames do anything the script called for. Photographing the flames was my responsibility. Though it presented problems, it also offered a very unusual opportunity. I immediately realized that flames could become an unusual element in presenting not only Rambo's solution to his predicament, but that the flames would let me do something unusual with the photography.

Our set, three stories high, was built in an enormous warehouse outside of Vancouver, British Columbia. It was a truly beautiful set. It had interesting rock formations, constantly dripping water everywhere, lakes, an underground river, tiny crevasses and large open areas for Rambo to traverse, while trying to find his way out of the cave. I felt that lighting the cave, though it could have produced photographically pleasing images, would have been wrong. The director, Ted Kotcheff, agreed. But when I mentioned it to the producer of the film, he felt, quite rightfully, I must add, that he spent hundreds of thousands of dollars building the set and didn't want to jeopardize paying it off, as one of the large production values of the film. My contention was that the audience should see and experience the cave the same way as Rambo does, by having elements, surprises, such as a pack of rats, be unexpectedly brought into view by the light of Rambo's torch. I also felt that choreographing Rambo's actions with the torch would create unusual, beautiful images. I was convinced the film would greatly benefit from using the torch as our sole source of light. Lighting a three-story set with the flame of one torch wasn't an easy sell, but in the end everyone bought the idea. The finished film turned out immensely better off for it.

The writer needs to put these kinds of details into the script if he knows them; otherwise, leave these details to the DP who's better qualified to supply the technical and creative solutions to problems. The author should write that Rambo is lost in the cave and then fashions a torch which shows him the way out—that's all. I used those elements and bent them to enhance the visual aspects of the scene. In the case of *First Blood*, the writer, being concerned with the story line, did supply the details regarding the importance of the torch, but I don't believe he could've foreseen the importance of the torch as an element of lighting.

Tobias: From your point of view, when does a writer's input become superfluous?

Laszlo: When writers get carried away with describing shots in extensive detail, it interferes with the reading of the script, the continuity, and the flow of the story. In most cases the writing is going to be subject to interpretation. In fact, in more than a few cases I've been witness to hard feelings that can develop between writers and producers. Writers are invited to the set or have a contractual right to be there and when they see a director is deviating from their vision, at times they object. At times a writer may protest and in some extreme cases even remove his name from the project or inititate a lawsuit. Unless the writer's input is extremely important to him, the final look should be left to the director and the cinematographer.

Tobias: Are you saying that a little description goes a long way?

Laszlo: It is best if the writer leaves a little area so that the director and the DP aren't locked into rigid guidelines. Let's say the writer says something about an eerie blue light that permeates the set. The writer puts the idea in my mind. I ask myself, what is an eerie light? Would it have color? If so, what color? Why is it necessary? What is it going to do? I either accept it or I don't, but it's going to be hard to stop thinking about it because it's there in the script. I have to keep thinking about it. And if I do use a blue light or some other kind of light, my idea of what's eerie may not match the writer's vision.

On the other hand, if I felt that a scene could be helped with the addition of color, even though no such thing is called for in the script, I would put that in.

Tobias: How do you go about making your own creative decisions?

Laszlo: If I'm doing a picture, by the time it goes to photography, the blank backside of every page of the script is full of notes of what I have to do with that particular scene. It is full of ideas about where and how and what equipment I need, and what to and what not to do. A director's script looks the same.

Tobias: How much should a writer put in a script in terms of camera shots?

Laszlo: The writer should try to convey his visual image. If he or she feels strongly that a medium shot should be used in that scene, then say so. It may not be accepted, but it should be noted. Take the bathroom scene in Stanley Kubrick's *The Shining*, for example. The description of the scene says that the young woman being pursued by her mad husband locks herself in the bathroom. That's all the description you need. If there should be an extreme closeup of the door knob turning, indicating that her nemesis is outside trying to get in, then that shot should also be noted. A good director gets those little cuts that sell suspense and create tension whether they're listed in the writer's version of the script or not. But only if it's extremely important. Look at *Jaws* by Spielberg. It's full of thousands of little cuts that could never have been all listed in the screenplay. These details shouldn't be in the script.

Tobias: What do you look for when you read a script?

Laszlo: Recently a studio sent me a script to read which was the first effort of a young screenwriter. I started reading it and twenty pages into the script, I picked up the phone in New York and called the film's producer in Los Angeles because it was the most fantastic, the best written script I'd ever read. The writing style was so wonderful that I just couldn't contain myself.

The story wasn't unique—it was a Godfather-type movie—so it wasn't the story. But the writing was fresh. And witty. That's the first thing I look for. How much I like or dislike the story. The second thing I look for is who will be in the picture, who is directing, who is producing, what the budget is, you know, what the potential of the picture is. Then I look to see what I can do to make the picture photographically interesting or unique. How can I enhance the story to make it more interesting, more memorable than it is on the written page? Which is very difficult. The written page allows one to use one's imagination as a reader. If somebody gives you a description, let's say, about the smoke coming out of Yellowstone Park during the great forest fires of 1988, and you've never witnessed such an event, you may have a vivid picture in your mind. But if I create the image on film, that will be the only image an audience will see. They will either accept or reject it. So I look for opportunities to enhance what my interpretation is of the written scene.

When I first read *Shogun* I didn't have any idea I'd wind up with the motion picture project. It was one of the greatest novels I'd ever read. Everything jumped off the page even though I didn't know what a real Japanese kimono looked like or what a Japanese castle looked like. Yet the opportunities were there to improve and to enhance. Just the selection of the focal length of a lens or whether a shot should be done in back light or front light is an enhancement.

Tobias: Do you try to make your point of view the same as the writer's?

Laszlo: The script is a blueprint, not a bible. The blueprint contains all the elements necessary for the structure to be erected. I deal with the overall and the detail within the overall. The writer's script is a departure point. I have to carry on, and at the end, when the picture is shown for the first time, it's my name there that says director of photography, and I have to stand by what I put on the film—good, bad, or indifferent. So if I accept the writer's work and do things that are my interpretation of what he might have been thinking, that could be completely wrong. But it's better if the picture is entirely my interpretation of what I thought. You can't be going in fifteen different directions at once, but at the same time you have to bring your own individuality to the photography. If you don't, every picture would look like every other picture.

Tobias: Talk more about the process of interpreting the written word into an image.

Laszlo: I read a script and try to imagine what the writer's description might look like. Let's say there is a scene with a truck towing a trailer. It makes a wrong turn and cuts off a car that then turns over. All this is in the script. But what will the scene end up looking like? The process of interpretation is a difficult one. When you go visit the proposed location where the accident is to take place, all kinds of considerations come into play. First of all, is it possible to stage and photograph the accident there? And that's not just my opinion. A lot of other people are going to visit all the possible location sites. Everybody is going to have some input. The stunt coordinator, for example, might say, "Well, the stunt is either not going to work here or it's not going to be spectacular enough. There should be a hillside for the car to roll down." The script never said anything about the car rolling down a hillside, but there's a stuntman who thinks it should roll down a hillside and maybe even burst into flames at the bottom of the hill. His major interest is not necessarily in what the script says. He knows there's an accident and he's going to try to stage it in the most spectacular manner. The producer may counter and say, "There's nothing in the script that says that the car rolls down a hillside, nor it is important to the story. As long as it rolls over, that's all we're interested in." Then I come in and say, "Well, the accident is supposed to take place in the Rockies surrounded by beautiful scenery and mountains and this looks like a street corner in New Jersey." What I'm saying is that I don't like it. If I thought the location was mundane or didn't bring anything extraordinary to that bit of action or the story, or I thought the location wasn't interesting enough, I wouldn't favor it and would suggest that we look elsewhere. That's my input. Every scene has to be considered individually. But then when every scene is considered, the overall has to be considered too. In other words, is this bit of action going to be so spectacular that everything before and after it is going to look mundane? Or is it going to be so totally mundane that everything before and after it is going to look more interesting than the accident. This isn't the writer's job; it's mine.

Tobias: In *The Warriors*, the script says nothing about a rain storm, yet there's one in the picture. Why did you do that?

Laszlo: The entire story takes place during one night in New York. It took us seventy-six consecutive nights to film it. During one of the early production meetings, I asked what would happen if we arrived on one of our locations and it rained? We had no covered sets to go to and I wanted to know what the studio's policy was concerning rain days. It was certainly possible that it would rain at least one night in New York over a period of seventy-six consecutive nights. Maybe it was obvious, but nobody had thought of it. The screenwriter certainly hadn't. He was focused on one night. But if it did start raining, then we would have to stand down for the evening, and that would cost the production half a million dollars. So I suggested that at one scene early in the film we stage a tremendous thunderstorm. Once we'd staged the downpour, the streets could be wet for the rest of the film. So if it rains, it rains. We brought in equipment to wet down every scene, and even though it was expensive, the loss of one night's work would've been far more costly. Wetting down the streets also helped the picture photographically. It created beautiful reflections in what otherwise would have been featureless, black pavement.

Tobias: Do you think the screenwriter has the responsibility to think about those kinds of contingencies?

Laszlo: If he does, it's a real plus, but realistically, the only thing the writer is responsible for is the story. He should leave the logistics to the large crew of experts whose job it is to deal with them. I'm one of them.

Chapter Eight

Inside the Screenwriter

When I first started to outline this book, I made a conscious decision not to interview screenwriters. My reasoning was pretty straightforward. If you want interviews with screenwriters, the bookstore is full of them. I didn't think I could add anything more to the already prodigious volume of screenwriter interviews out there.

An Interview With Thomas McGuane

I changed my mind because of Tom McGuane. Tom is best known as a writer of both fiction and nonfiction. He's a master craftsman who's published many novels and countless articles and short stories. Tom has crossed the line between literary fiction and nonfiction over into film both as a screenwriter (*Missouri Breaks*) and as a director (*92 in the Shade*). Very rarely do you find a person well practiced in several arts.

More importantly, I was interested in the difference between writing a novel or a short story and writing a screenplay. Because Tom has also directed, he understands better than most the connections that are necessary between writer, director and actor.

Tobias: When you wrote your first screenplay, what kinds of changes did you have to make in terms of attitude and writing style?
McGuane: Screenwriting is very structure related, compared to novels. Novels move forward purely on atmosphere and characters and rarely will that work with screenplays. The screenplay is a more narrative form than fiction writing. When you write for the screen, you can't supply a lot of the techniques you're obliged to supply in novels that allow you to focus on the real armature of the story. Later, when I directed *92 in the Shade*, I found that screenplays are better when they suggest rather than state.

Tobias: Explain what you mean by "suggest."

McGuane: In a novel, you try to control everything that happens in the reader's mind. That's not strictly true, but certainly more so than in a screenplay. The screenwriter very soon must realize that he is just one of the contributors to this artifact. Once you know that you can't change that, then you try to strategize the space. You try to take a key place in each scene rather than paint each scene by the numbers.

Tobias: Can you give an example?

McGuane: Let's say you have had a simple moment. Someone is at home watching television and somebody walks into the room who the person watching television doesn't know. The scene is now obligated to go in certain directions because the people don't know each other. Then you add the fact that the guy is carrying a gun. Then the scene has yet another direction. In a novel you would enumerate all the things that could or would happen, but in a screenplay you leave a lot of that unsaid because a lot of what is going to happen will be nonverbal. But you try to take up the positions in the scenes and control the direction it goes without describing everything that happens. It becomes a skeleton in a sense, but very deliberate. It's like the fall line for a skier. If you're going to ski down this hill, then you should cross these various points as you get to the bottom, but how you cross those points is going to be up to the skier.

Tobias: And those points are structural points?

McGuane: They could be atmosphere or character points, but basically they're structural. As a novelist you can do things that are purely part of your own quirkiness and persona. You can't do that in a screenplay.

Tobias: Do you have an audience in mind when you write a screenplay?

McGuane: I assume the audience and I have similar interests or similar capacities for surprise or similar demands on originality. I guess I try to write the movie I would like to see.

Tobias: So you're saying you make your audience come to you rather than you going to an audience?

McGuane: I think so. I wouldn't know how to write a Schwarzenegger movie. I admire someone who knows how to do that.

Movies aren't particularly human. They're products. I remember when I was at drama school, I had to write a play and then have it produced. The tension of this was beyond anything I've ever experienced since, because you're sitting in the audience and you realize that things are getting kind of boring. The play isn't going anywhere. For some reason audiences have a structural expectation. They'll let you tell them what the expectation should be. Screenwriters shouldn't lie to themselves about this because they'll go nowhere unless they get this point straight. An audience knows right away when something isn't working. A screenplay has to have a clear sense of cause-and-effect relationships that propel the story forward.

I recommend that you read your screenplay aloud with others around. Even in such a small community of viewers/listeners, they'll give you a pretty quick idea of what's not working.

Tobias: What about matters of style. As a fiction writer you have a reputation for your distinct style and voice. Do you incorporate them into your screenplays? Or do you strip those things out or hold them back?

McGuane: You strip them out. There should be a kind of angularity to anything you write. In a funny way, style becomes more and more subdued in good writing. Chekhov is so styleless and yet finally it is stylishness. Film is particularly hard on stylishness as we know it in the literary sense because you really don't want the author's presence. You really don't want him there puppeteering. The events are supposed to seem free floating.

Tobias: Do you find that frustrating or liberating?

McGuane: I find it fairly liberating. You don't have to worry about those things as you become a middle-aged writer. You're not interested in imposing your style on people. You want to get the thing done. Young writers are more interested in questions of style, and I always end up having to say to them, "You know, you've got that covered. Now let's write about something. Let's have a topic here. Let's just go on now if we may." As you get older, you concern yourself with style less and less. Look at a long career like Updike. He becomes less style oriented with each book. He's become almost a non-style.

Tobias: So the story is everything?

McGuane: It has to go straight to story. Ask yourself, "How are you going to get [style] through that many layers. How are you going to get through to the director or the producer? How are you going to get it through the actors, who are really the owners of cinema?"

Tobias: Why are actors the real owners of cinema?

McGuane: Movie directors aren't the stars anymore. Who knows who the directors are now? Ten years ago, in the last gasp of the auteur period (when the director had artistic control of his film so that it carried his individual imprint), people kind of knew. But directors are like us screenwriters now. They're just people who give material to the movie stars. Now you hear things like "This is a great character, but we don't think it's the sort of character who would interest a major movie star."

Tobias: What advice would you give a screenwriter?

McGuane: First, I'd suggest they not attempt to do the cameraman's job or the director's job. They should simplify their format. I've got mine down to exterior, interior, angle. A lot of apprentice screenwriters try to write everything. How the camera moves, everything. You know it's a chore for directors and producers to even read a screenplay. So you ought to be pretty austere at this level.

Second, I think in the course of every screenplay, there ought to be a point that the author recognizes, at which he can state plainly, what the picture is about.

Tobias: Something as simple as a premise, maybe?

McGuane: Something as simple as "What is this about?" There is a lot of coalescing of foggy materials in the beginning of a script that has to become purposeful. At that point you ought to be able to look back at Act I and see whether it has any grain, an internal antithesis. The story has to take us somewhere. I love westerns because it's so easy to see the grain in them. Westerns rely largely on social conditions. You have some individuals and then some problems arise between them and then you have your story.

I don't want to get into a dopey, anti-art posture here, because there are great movies that are hard to understand, but exceptions notwithstanding, you should be able to tell what a movie's about a third of the way through.

Watch films like *The Elephant Man*, *The Wild Bunch* and *Monsieur Hulot's Holiday*. And any of Buster Keaton's films.

Tobias: A novelist generally has full control of his work. How do you deal with the issue of your relative lack of control over your work as a screenwriter?

McGuane: You've got to have a policy about it. And probably a new policy every time you write a script. One thing I've found out is that if you want to stay and tough it out, you can. Producers and directors have the same ambiguous relationship to us as we have to them. It's just that most writers have a take-the-money-and-run attitude. They don't want to stay during production and fight with actors and directors. If you do want to stay around, they think they can get new scenes out of you and get their lines improved. So you can trade their need for you and try to influence the thing. I'm not sure it's worth doing because finally you won't have the power of a veto. But you can make them very nervous by being on the set. When they change lines they'll come back to you for reassurance and say, "What do you think? Don't you think that really was an improvement?" And if you say, "No, it's much worse," they get very nervous.

Tobias: Have any of your scripts been subjected to a rewriter?

McGuane: Just one. *The Missouri Breaks*. Arthur Penn wanted some changes which I considered really not in the best interest of the film, and I wouldn't do them. Actually it was Jack Nicholson who wanted the changes. There is a moment at the end where he shoots the girl's father. Nicholson felt that Brando got to go through all of this wild, emotional stuff and he had to stay restrained, so he wanted to go nuts at the end of the movie. I didn't want Jack to do that, so Penn brought in Robert Towne (*Chinatown*, *Tequila Sunrise*) and had him change the end. They really screwed up the film. People have agreed about that ever since.

Tobias: How do you reconcile it when a stranger comes in and significantly alters your story?

McGuane: At the time you feel terrible. At the time I was in great pain over what they were doing. They said, "Well, you can change it or we'll get somebody else to change it." But it's getting better now. The way to make things better is to get paid better. The more money you get, the more power you've got. And screenwriters were always pitifully paid compared to the other elements of the movie. Especially when you realize that the screenwriter made the whole thing up to start with. Screenwriters should get as much as the highest paid elements in any movie. They make the biggest contribution.

Tobias: As much as the six-million-dollar actors?

McGuane: John Grisham just sold the movie rights to his last book for six million dollars. Everybody's doing this tremendous gyration. Six million dollars! But those same people are very comfortable with Mel Gibson getting six million for showing up for six weeks of work. Screenwriters should be getting more than the movie stars. And at that moment, they'll be at the correct relationship in the power structure of a film.

Tobias: Mel Gibson is a bankable star. How many writers can draw people to the box office?

McGuane: I don't know, but I do know that you can't bank a movie without a screenwriter. You can bank one without a movie star, though. It's the one big, irreducible thing. Unless things have changed drastically in the last few months, you can't put together the elements of a film in the first place without a screenplay. You can't go to a studio and say, "We're going to make a Bruce Willis-Julia Roberts film. We don't have a screenplay. We're just going to make it." As powerful as they are, I don't think you could make one that way.

Tobias: When you write, do you have any real sense of the cost of production? Is that a necessary consideration for a writer?

McGuane: You should have some consciousness of it. The script I've just written is set in the twenties. I know it's an expensive concept to start with. There's a gleefulness about spending money in the movies on everybody's part. Sometimes you find yourself writing something that you know is an elaborate stunt or calls for a lot of construction. I directed a film, and I remember this weird feeling I got when we stopped traffic through a whole town during a shoot. Once you've been through a production and you know what things cost, you develop a sense of metering the bang for the buck as you go. If you do something that really doesn't have a lot to do with the advancement of the idea or the story and you know it's enormously expensive, then you're liable not to write that. Let's say you have a casual meeting between two characters set up in a diner, or you could dress it up a bit and set the scene on the Queen Mary. Both scenes have the same dialogue; it could happen in either place. You might want to cut the Queen Mary because of what you know about budgets.

Tobias: We have the old view of the writer as a passive person who sends off his manuscript and then patiently waits for an answer. But now you hear about a new generation of writers who are aggressive and find ways to get their scripts read. Do you find this to be true?

McGuane: Yes. The old concept of behavior came out of publishing, when we used to have wonderful, old, idealistic houses. Scribners, Harcourt, companies run by people who really wanted to find some good stuff to publish. The writer's only problem was to write well. Then, if it was good, the publishers would find it. That's a kind of structure for fair-minded people. We don't have that in the movie industry. No one really wants material of real quality that would improve our national body of literature. So, if you want to be in this corrupt business—as so many of us do—then you have to take on some of the corruption and be a bit of a salesman. You have to go out there and advocate your own stuff. You can't afford to sit and wait and hope you'll be discovered anymore.

Chapter Nine

Inside the Agent

In terms of love-hate relationships, the agent tops the list. No one is so universally loved or despised as an agent. Nor is it black and white that you either hate or love your agent; instead you actively hate and love him/her/them/it at any given moment in the day. People who are normally stoic and calm will suddenly flash through a range of emotions when talk turns to representation.

Agents are a mysterious lot. Everybody knows what they do and yet nobody knows what they do. They're experts at the coddle, the nurse, the nudge and the push. They're masters at the feint, the sleight and the dodge. They know their client's weak and strong spots and how to bolster both.

Good agents are the very definition of slick. They're endearing without being ingratiating, yet they can tell you to go to hell and make you want to go. They have Rolodexes that most of us would kill for, and yet we know that such a vast archive of phone numbers would be totally worthless in our hands. So what if you have Arnold Schwarzenegger's phone number? He's not going to talk to you or me. But he will talk to an agent.

Not only do they tell their clients what they should do, but also what they shouldn't do. They are guardians of their client's image, projects, and pocketbook. Agents are handlers. They handle egos, mainly. And if there's one town in which the egos are huge, it's Hollywood.

Agents represent primarily people and things. Actors, directors, and producers fall under the category of people. Writers, on the other hand, fall under the category of things. That sounds awful, but it isn't meant to be derogatory. Writers produce scripts, and scripts are the things that agents represent. Therefore, an agent who represents you, really represents the property you have created, the focus of everything. The script, after all, is the foundation upon which all deals are made. The decision to make a movie is based on three things: the property, the calendar and the money. But it all starts with the property. Yes, it is true that writers sometimes become important enough to be classified as people (when someone wants to commission a writer to write a script), but most of us will never escape the category of "commodity."

The point of this chapter is to give you an insight into how an agent thinks. The agent's point of view is different from that of any of the other people in this book, and if you want a screenplay that will appeal to an agent, then knowing the mind of an agent is as important as knowing the mind of a producer or director. Perhaps more than any other person, the agent is concerned with movies as a business.

An Interview With Jack Gilardi

International Creative Management is a who's who of Hollywood's elite. Among the pantheon of top-flight agencies, it is a force to be reckoned with. Their client list is the cream of the crop, including both top-flight established and up-and-coming talent. Jack Gilardi, executive vice-president of ICM, represents some of the biggest names in the business. His long experience with the agency makes him one of Hollywood's true veterans.

Tobias: What is the prime consideration in your mind when you read a script?

Gilardi: Its commercial value, no question. The cost of pictures today is so exorbitant that you'd like to get your investment back. Nobody can tell you what the audience is going to accept or reject or think about or not think about. So our business is really driven by the name of an actor in a picture. When I look for material for Jean-Claude Van Damme, I get a lot of action scripts. So I have to figure out which action has been done and overdone and redone and rehashed and not hashed. I look for something different. When I look for material for Robert Mitchum or Charlton Heston or Shelley Winters, I look for material that complements them as actors.

There are three ways to read a script. On the one hand, some of my associates read a script because a studio has committed to it, and they want to figure out which of our clients might be right for the roles. On the other hand, other of our associates read scripts for their clients—whether it be Mel Gibson or Arnold Schwarzenegger—because they're primarily involved with those clients. Those scripts may not have a commitment to a studio yet.

A third way of reading a script entails independent production. A lot of independent pictures don't have all the money put together yet. So I'll read a script from a different point of view. I ask myself, "What is the budget of the picture? Who's going to direct it? What is its commercial value?" Then I'll package it together into a whole. So there are three different approaches or attitudes we might take to a script.

Tobias: Do you agree with the philosophy of some people who think a screenwriter should tailor the script for a particular lead actor or director?

Gilardi: Let me give you an example of how that kind of thinking can backfire. There's a very important writer in town who wrote a screenplay. The studio felt that the screenplay should be for a particular client of ours. The author was very upset by the suggestion. Not because he didn't like the actor, but because he thought that actor wasn't right for his screenplay. He wanted the role for a Harrison Ford or a Tom Cruise, rather than an action actor. It's a wonderful screenplay and the writer did a terrific job, but he wrote it having someone else in mind. The writer has to write a character that's good for the story. He can write with somebody in mind, but when the director gets the script or the studio gets it, they could say, "Yeah, if you make a change here, it could be right for . . . nope, forget it, we'll use a woman, and make a woman do the lead." You never know how it's going to play.

Tobias: How well versed should a writer be in terms of what things cost in production—a day scene versus a night scene, crowd scenes, period pieces, and so forth?

Gilardi: The writer should write the best story possible. They can always take out the forty-two crashes. They can always take out the forty-two explosions. If the basic story is there, it'll work. I think the underlying philosophy is let's not worry about what the budget is going to be, let's worry about what the story is going to be.

Tobias: There's a writer out there in Iowa City, Iowa. He's just written his first screenplay. He doesn't know what to do with it. The obvious thing to do is send it to an agent. But a friend says, "Don't go to an agent. Find a way to capture a director or a producer in a cab. Corner him in the dentist's chair if you have to, but get to that person. Then try to attach a couple names to it and build from that." What's your reaction to that kind of approach?

Gilardi: That's a great philosophy but it has its problems. Years ago the studios ran the business of motion pictures because they had actors under contract. Warner Brothers had its list, MGM had its list, and

Columbia had its list of players. If it was Paramount, it had Barbara Stanwyck and Robert Ryan; Universal had Robert Mitchum and Warners used Mr. Cagney, Mr. Bogart and Mr. Robinson week after week. "You be the bad guy this week. I'll be the good guy."

My point is the studios controlled the business. Agents were like nursemaids. Today the agents are more in control because the agents represent the talent. Whether it's ICM or CAA or William Morris, they represent the writers, directors and actors.

In our country we're driven by name actors. Those are the ones they put on the marquee. Very seldom do they put the writer's name. Very seldom do they put the director's name. So to get to an actor these days is very difficult. It's very difficult for a writer from Iowa City to come to Hollywood and give a screenplay to an actor or a director of importance. Even studio executives are hesitant to accept unsolicited material.

Tobias: It sounds like agents are doing now what the studios were doing fifty years ago.

Gilardi: Somewhat, yes.

Tobias: How many scripts does your office get in an average week?

Gilardi: About thirty scripts a week. Three-quarters of them are solicited and the other quarter are not. Sometimes they're not registered with the Writers Guild, so we return them and say, "Thank you very much, but we can't look at it."

Tobias: Why can't you look at scripts that aren't registered with the Writers Guild?

Gilardi: Let's say we read a script that hasn't been registered with the Writers Guild, and then another script that is registered with the Guild comes in that has a similar theme. We read them both and send the first script back. The second script is much better. Five years down the line the first guy sues us saying, "I sent you a script that you rejected and yet you stole my idea and made a movie from it." That's why we have to be very careful.

Tobias: What about market analysis? A few years ago you could see that *Dances With Wolves* was opening the gate for westerns. Do you recommend writers to start thinking that way or should they just write the best stories they know how?

Gilardi: A writer should only write the best story he or she knows how. I don't think there are such things as trends. For five minutes there's a good reason why people copy. "Oh, God, let's see. We had one western, *Dances With Wolves*. Let's make *Wyatt Earp*. Let's make *Tombstone*." Unfortunately a couple of bad pictures kills the western theater because too many people are trying to cash in on it.

Tobias: What about the writer who does want to write a western now?

Gilardi: A writer has to write what he feels. It might not be the correct work for today, it might not be the trend today, it might not be a comedy for today, but I believe that if a writer produces a great screenplay, it will attract somebody and be made.

Tobias: What about roles for women? There are a lot of good actresses out there who can't find roles.

Gilardi: Meryl Streep has found some material that's been very good for women, but I agree, there hasn't been a lot of good material for women. I don't know why. Most writers write for leading men. Action, leading men. There should be an action woman star, but we haven't found the script, or a woman, to do that at the moment.

A lot of good women are coming into the business behind the camera, whether it be Barbra Streisand or Betty Thomas or Lee Grant. There are some very fine, bright, intelligent women who are good writers. Nora Ephron. Good writers and directors. Eventually there will be more starring roles for women. Women-driven roles for Julia Roberts or Ellen Barkin or Holly Hunter.

Tobias: What about women in starring roles on television?

Gilardi: There are a lot more roles for women in television than there are for men. Especially in the two-hour or four-hour-long form.

Tobias: What don't you like to see in the way a script is written in terms of camera or personal direction?

Gilardi: Personally I don't like reading direction in a script. The director is going to have to point the camera. He's going to say it's over on the left or on the right or out in front or "Give me some movement." Too much direction makes the script drag. It bogs down the story.

First-time writers want to impress the agent, the producer, the director or whoever with their knowledge of camera movements. They shouldn't do that. They're not going to tell a seasoned director who's going to take on an expensive picture how to do it.

Tobias: How do you screen scripts for a star?

Gilardi Usually readers or my assistants screen scripts for me. I only read the scripts that rise to the top of the pile. But when it comes to a star—let's say Jean-Claude Van Damme, who's very hot and getting hotter right now—I read everything. We live with Jean-Claude every day. We're trying to get better material for him. We don't want to go back to *Cyborg*. We are trying to elevate him from *Bloodsport* which was very good and really turned him around as an actor. That moved him up to *Universal Soldier* which was a bigger budget picture, bigger things to do, more challenging for him. That moved him up to a Joe Eszterhas script, *Nowhere to Run* with a better director (Robert Harmon). Now he's directing his first picture, *The Quest.* So you can see that we're always looking for scripts that allow Jean-Claude to grow and move forward.

Tobias: Do you think writers should stay at home during production or should they come onto the set?

Gilardi: It depends upon the story and the writer. You just don't arbitrarily make a rule and say, "No, the writer shouldn't go." In certain instances, the writer should go. It depends upon the writer and his dedication to the work.

I remember a long time ago (1963) John Cassavetes was directing a motion picture with Burt Lancaster and Judy Garland called *A Child is Waiting.* Abby Mann wrote the screenplay. Abby Mann is an Academy Award-winning writer. But as every writer, he didn't want a single word changed. An actor wants a word changed because of his feeling about how he will depict the character, make the character better. He doesn't feel comfortable with the line the author wrote, so he wants to say something else but maybe with the same meaning. Writers want their words to be in stone. And Abby Mann was all over John Cassavetes saying, "He [Burt Lancaster] changed a line. He changed a line." Cassavetes turned to Abby and said, "I'm barring you from the set."

Not all writers are like that, of course. Richard Attenborough wanted John Briley on the set of *Gandhi.* And if an actor had a problem with a particular line, they sat down and Briley said, "Let's correct it. Let's make it work. Let's make it right for the picture." So there are pictures where writers should be on set. But it should be the director's choice.

You can't tell a Richard Donner or an Ivan Reitman or Wolfgang Petersen or Bernardo Bertolucci what to do because they smell and feel and they have to put those words into a picture. They have to take and dramatize those words and make the actor perform them. The director is the real filmmaker. He takes the words from the writer and the performance from the actor and makes the film.

Tobias: Do you feel the balance of power shifting away from the director and toward the actor?

Gilardi: The actor is getting more strength, more voice about what they're doing, because the actor might be the one that triggers the picture and makes it go. If I got a fifty-million-dollar picture going and my star is having a bad time with the director, I'm going to side with the actor. Maybe he's not right, but I'm going to side with him. But if you've done your homework and have the right chemistry between the director, the writer and the actor, then you're not going to have problems. Did you ever hear of a problem on a Mel Gibson picture? Or an Arnold Schwarzenegger picture? No. You don't have really major problems with professional people.

This isn't anything new, either. When I was a young agent I saw John Wayne on location with Howard Hawks. John Wayne was the power in that relationship. Before Hawks would do anything he would say, "Is that okay, Duke?" If it wasn't, the Duke would say so. It was his face on that screen. His movement. The actor has the right to say, "I don't feel comfortable playing the scene this way."

Tobias: If you could speak directly to the writer, what advice would you give?

Gilardi: When I first started out there was a literary agent who told me something that has stuck ever since. He said, "If it's not on the page, it's not on the stage." The writer is the one that starts everything. That doesn't mean there won't be changes. But the script is the basic construction. Without the script, the director has nothing to direct and the actor has nothing to say.

But the writer needs to understand the collaborative process. You can't take the stand: "These are my words and this is what I want to sell to you, the director, and you, the actor." Because the actor will say, "Geez, I love the idea, but I've got to make changes because I feel it for me." And the director will say, "Yeah, but I visualize this, but I have an idea." If the writer says, "No way. Either you do it my way or you don't do it all," you'll end up at home with your screenplay. He might have had an opportunity if he'd let go and said, "OK, let's try it." It's tough, sure. It's a great business, and if you're talented and you believe in this business, it's wonderful.

Tobias: Is persistence still the best virtue?

Gilardi: Yes, but you must also have the talent.

DO YOU NEED AN AGENT?

Everyday untold thousands of writers seek the aid and comfort of an agent. Those who don't have one, want one; those who have one, want a bigger one or a better one. There's no place on earth that better proves the adage "The grass always seems greener on the other side of the hill." It's a hotbed industry; there's as much or perhaps more lateral movement as there is upward movement. Some clients, some of them very famous, act like fleas the way they hop from agent to agent, agency to agency.

Names are important. You are definitely judged by the agent you keep.

There are all kinds of agents, and there are all kinds of agencies. You shouldn't necessarily get depressed because you have a no-name agent at a no-name agency; it may very well be that person knows exactly where to take your script. And you shouldn't get too puffed up for having a big-name agent at a big-name agency either. That agent may be too busy with his big-name clients (who rake in a lot more dough for the agency than you ever will) to spend much time on small potatoes like you. Granted, the more powerful the agent and the more powerful the agency, the better the *overall* results.

There's a paradox at work here: Since an agent makes a commission only on sales, then the bottom line is your earning potential. A top actor can make $12-15 million on a single deal. A top screenwriter on a *really* good day, could take home $3 million. And $12-million acting deals are much more common than $3-million screenwriting deals. Consequently important agents at important agencies have less time to spend on potential writing talent, whereas smaller agencies have more time to spend, but less access to the movers and shakers in the industry.

Sure, it feels good to have a big-time agent at a big-time agency, but can you afford it? You don't want to end up a *pro bono* case at a hotshot agency; you want commitment, energy and enthusiasm from your agent. The problem is that good agents will seem to have these qualities at a moment's notice. The real test is results. The proof of the pudding, as we're fond of saying, is in the eating.

HOW TO GET YOUR OWN AGENT

Along you come with a script, looking for representation. How do you make your own pitch to an agent and how do you maintain a good working relationship with an agent once you have one? The following five-step procedure offers answers to these questions.

Step One: The List

The first commandment when it comes to finding an agent: Call or write the Writer's Guild and ask for a list of agencies that have agreed to abide by Working Rule 23, "No writer shall enter into a representation agreement, whether oral or written, with any agent who has not entered into an agreement with the Guild covering minimum terms and conditions between agents and their writer clients." Chances are you're not a member of the Guild (more on how to join the Guild in chapter eleven); that means you're free to choose whatever agent you want, but you would be unwise to deal with any agent who isn't on that list. Agents that are on the Guild's list have a standard code of conduct in terms of what they charge you (10 percent) and what they charge others on your behalf. Think of it as protection. If you've been contacted by an agent who's new in the business and tells you that he/she isn't a member of the Guild *yet*, but plans to join, be very wary. My suggestion is to deal only with agencies that are already members.

Step Two: The Angle

You've got the Writer's Guild list of agents in your hand. The next step is to try to decide which agent will suit you best.

The best approach is through a personal connection, preferably a writer who already has an agent. Be direct, but go easy. First, ask your friend if he'd be willing to read your script.

If he says, "I'd really like to but I just don't have any time," be polite, thank him, and then try to find someone else. If he says, "Sure, but I'm really swamped with work right now. It might take me awhile," you shoud respond, "Fine. Take your time. I really want some professional input."

If your friend does agree to read your script, *be patient*. You might have to twiddle your thumbs for four, six or eight weeks. Don't harass your friend with phone calls, just wait for his response.

It may seem like forever, but your friend will finally read your script and get back to you. Listen carefully. What is your friend really saying? Are you being damned with faint praise? Or is the praise genuine? Your friend's reply may address problems in the script. If you agree with the criticism, then start thinking about a rewrite.

If, however, your friend thinks the work is really good, then push forward. Ask, "How would you feel about recommending me to your agent?" A genuine recommendation from someone the agent knows and respects is as good an entree as you're going to get.

Odds are you may not know a screenwriter you can ask. Then what do you do?

Look at that list of agents from the Guild. Don't waste your time with a blanket approach by sending letters to everyone on the list asking them if they want another client. It's a waste of time and stamps. Sort through the information.

WHICH AGENTS WILL READ UNSOLICITED SCREEN-PLAYS? These agencies are looking for up-and-coming talent, and they might be willing to read your script based on how well you can entice them with a query letter (more on that later). The downside to this approach is that everyone else in the universe looking for an agent also knows this and chances are the agent is inundated with requests to read scripts. You need a really good query letter to break through.

WHAT ABOUT AGENTS WHO WON'T READ UNSOLIC-ITED SCREENPLAYS? As a producer, I learned a long time ago that just because people say they won't give you money doesn't mean they really won't give you money. In fact, I learned it's easier to get money from people who say they won't give it to you than from people who say they will. I know that sounds like a paradox, but there's a logic to it. If I announce myself as a financial source, then everyone who needs a buck will be pounding on my door. It's hard to break through that chaos. Agents would shoot me for saying this, but just because they say they won't read unsolicited manuscripts doesn't necessarily mean they won't. You don't know until you try. But if you do try, make sure you have a good reason for hitting on that agency, maybe it represents writers who write like you do.

How can you find out which writers are with which agency? Pay attention to end credits of shows you admire. Write down the name of the writer(s) or the story editor (in the case of television). When you have three names, call the Writers Guild, West (WGAW) and ask for the "Agency Department." They'll tell you which agency represents those writers. Don't call with a big list of names: They'll only answer three queries.

Once you have an angle, make your approach.

Step Three: The Approach

You're talking to salespeople, and *you've got to sell yourself.* The traditional way is to send a query letter.

First, the "don'ts."

DON'T BE NEGATIVE. "I'm just an unknown, struggling writer and I've written a screenplay I think is pretty good. . . ."

DON'T BE OUTRAGEOUS. "I'm the best damn screenwriter you'll ever read. . . ."

DON'T LIE. "I've written several screenplays and done network television and would like a new agent. . . ." Or "Robert Towne is a good friend of mine and he said. . . ."

DON'T SEND YOUR SCREENPLAY(S). Never send your work until someone asks you to send it.

DON'T BE TOO INFORMAL OR TOO FORMAL. "Hey. . . ." or "Dear Sir or Madam. . . ." Get names. Talk to real people, not to the agency. Decide if you'd rather speak to a woman or a man. (Maybe you feel your material is more suited to one sex than to the other.)

DON'T GET LONG-WINDED. Time is money and you're on the clock. Be clear and to the point. Don't be too businesslike, but don't get too chatty.

You want to strike a balance between professionalism and friendliness. Don't give your life story. Stick to the matter at hand: I have a screenplay, and it's about. . . . Let a touch of your personality come through. How? Through style or wit; but remember, a little goes a long way. Keep your letter to one page. The shorter the better: You're trying to set the hook, not reel in a catch.

And, the "do's."

BE CREATIVE. If your letter is dreary, don't expect an enthusiastic response. Don't go overboard being creative; don't get cute or silly. The point is that you're claiming to be a writer, and you're writing to an agent. The agent sees your letter as evidence of your skill (or lack of it). If the letter is engaging, the agent will respond; if it's not, then why bother reading your script? You've already proven you can't write.

The best way to approach the problem is to consider it from the agent's point of view. It's 9 AM and you've just gotten your first cup of coffee. The clerk comes in and delivers the morning mail. It's a daunting pile—fifty, maybe sixty letters. Most of them are "You don't know me but I've just written a screenplay" letters from aspiring writers. The phone rings; you have a 9:30 meeting with a client. You open the first letter. "Hello, I've just written a screenplay about. . . . Would you like to read it?" You spend maybe fifteen seconds on the letter, and then you open the next one. . . . Forty-nine more letters are waiting for replies.

That's how it is. So you have to do something that seizes the attention of the reader, something that says, "This letter isn't like the other forty-nine letters you have read this morning; this letter is different, and my story is worth reading."

How do you do that?

I'll give you an example, but by the time you're finished reading it, the idea will be stale. You'll have to figure out your own approach. Creativity is always fresh; if you do what everyone else is doing, then you're just part of the herd.

Rob had a stroke of genius. He'd just finished a screenplay about a woman who worked in a phone-sex parlor. Instead of taking the standard approach, he wrote the letter from the point of view of his main character, Lisa. He wrote in what would've been Lisa's style and manner. He even included a real phone-sex number. At the bottom of the letter he added a postscript that said Lisa was a fictional character and gave his real name.

Rob sent out ten letters to agents he thought might be interested in the script. Out of ten letters, you'd be lucky to get one or two positive responses. Rob got nine. Nine agents called on the phone and said they'd like to read his script. One even asked for Lisa by name.

I tried the technique myself about a year later to see if it was a fluke. I sent out ten letters: I got eight positive replies.

By the time you read this, the technique might not work anymore. Anyway, you can see how it breaks through the sameness of the crowd. What is fresh without being silly or condescending is creative. The task falls to you as a creative person to come up with a fresh approach. Otherwise, you're just one more faceless grunt in a long line of writers making the same claims about their work.

SIGN THE RELEASE FORM. A release form states that the agent cannot be held legally accountable if a story like yours should suddenly show up on the screen after yours has been rejected. Every writer thinks his or her own ideas are unique and that no one else is thinking along the same lines. So if you were to send in a script about a friendly visitor from another planet to an agent and she sends it back saying, "Thanks, but no thanks," and next year a film shows up in your local theater by Steven Spielberg called *E.T.*, then you're likely to see your lawyer. (This actually happened.) Agents want to be protected legally as much as anyone else. If an agent requests that you sign a release form, don't get paranoid and start dreaming of plots to steal your work. The request is a matter-of-course; don't make any fuss about it.

PACKAGE YOUR CONCEPT. You used to hear the phrase "elevator time" in writer's circles. For those of you who have ever had to make a pitch, you learn very quickly that time is of the essence. "Elevator time" meant that you had as much time to present your story as it took for an elevator to go from the first to the eleventh floor. Two minutes, max. There's a prevalent belief that if you can't present your idea in a convincing and entertaining way in 120 seconds, then no amount of time will help. A fly-fisherman knows that presentation of the bait is as important as the bait itself, and so it is with pitching your idea.

This thinking gave way to "high concept," which is as much a curse as it is a blessing. High concept took the idea of elevator time and reduced it even further. The main premise behind high concept is that you should be able to pitch your idea *in a single sentence*. And a short sentence at that. What if somebody brought back dinosaurs from their DNA? (*Jurassic Park*.) What if something *really* went wrong on a moon mission? (*Apollo 13*.) It got so bad that you could pitch a concept simply by referring to another movie. *Die Hard* on a plane (*Passenger 57*); *Die Hard* on a boat (*Under Siege*); *Die Hard* on a bus (*Speed*) and *Die Hard* on a train (*Under Siege 2*). (What's left: *Die Hard* in a taxi?)

High concept is great for getting somebody's immediate attention, but the downside of high concept is that the heart of the film must be reduced to such a low common denominator. High concept clearly favors action-oriented plots as opposed to stories that are more subtle and complex, typical of character-oriented plots. There are many great films that if they were reduced to a single plot line would sound downright idiotic: What if two men had dinner together? (*My Dinner With Andre*.) What if an eighty-year-old man and his wife and daughter spend a holiday at their lakeside cottage? (*On Golden Pond*.) What if a mute woman on her way to an arranged marriage has to leave her piano on the beach? (*The Piano*.) What if a young boy makes friends with the projectionist at the theater? (*Cinema Paradiso*.) Those films would never have sold on the basis of a one-line premise.

Your time is limited in your query letter, too. If your letter is long and drawn out or if you can't find a handle to aptly characterize your film and capture the imagination of the reader, then you're handicapping yourself. It may be that your film lends itself to this kind of condensation, but then again, your story may resist being stuffed into a one-line premise. Do the best you can. If you can't come up with a one-line description, then come up with a teaser that will make the agent want to read your script.

PACKAGE YOURSELF. An agent prefers long-term relationships to one-script stands. An agent will be more interested in you if you indicate you have other scripts besides the one you're pitching. You should also indicate that your script(s) can be used as examples of your writing talent. This attitude will indicate to the agent that you're open to compromise and that you have realistic expectations about getting work.

Include a very brief description of any information you think would make you more appealing to the agent. Agents also tend to prefer people who are readily available to "take" meetings. If you live in South Dakota, it isn't feasible for you to show up for a meeting, but you should indicate your willingness to travel to L.A. if necessary. Or maybe you make several trips to California each year.

The prejudice for people who live in the area seems to be fading. A lot of Hollywood people don't even live in Hollywood anymore. "Name the day and time and I'll be there," is really all you have to say.

SHOW YOUR WILLINGNESS. Not only are you willing to work, but you're willing to work together with other people.

Step Four: The Acceptance

An agent calls: She wants to read your script. Sign the release if she requests it, send the script first class (there's no need to overnight it), and then sit tight. (Don't forget to register your script with the WGA before you send it in.) Indicate in your cover letter that you'd appreciate any feedback she could give.

If the agent likes your script, that's a major step forward for you. But don't just settle for the first agent that wants you. If another agent expresses interest, let him read it too. Find out from both agencies what other writers they represent and what they've written.

Getting an agent isn't just a matter of finding anyone who will take you, but finding the best possible person to take you. So many first-time writers are so happy at being accepted by someone that they don't care how good the agent or the agency is. They ride high for a while, but that good feeling tarnishes with time when nothing happens with the script. In the end, they've wasted a lot of precious time.

Do a little research: Who are these people? What kind of reputation do they have with writers? (I've always been suspicious of agents who refer to their roster of clients as their "stable" of writers. It makes me feel like a mule, or worse yet, a jackass.) Always be polite and prompt. Start a dialogue with your agent; become a real person rather than just a name. The phone is better than a letter; a visit is better than a phone call.

But don't become a pest; that's suicide. You'll have to strike a balance between too little presence and too much presence. The best way to impress your agent is to continue to write and send scripts. If you sit back and wait for your first script to sell, you might be sitting for a long time, and eventually your frustration will focus on your agent. Always move forward. A resting object loses momentum and becomes inert. An inert writer is worthless.

Step Five: The Agreement

When you do enter into a relationship with an agent, you will have to sign an agreement that protects both you and the agent. It lays out the terms of the relationship, including the charges for representing you. The standard fee for representation by an agency is 10 percent of any income the agent generates on your behalf. When it comes time for you to be paid, the money will be sent to the agent, who takes the agency's deduction, and then forwards the balance to you with a complete accounting, if necessary.

The burden of proof falls on the agent. If you sign a contract that is typical of WGA contracts between writers and agents, then the agent has ninety days in which to sell your work. If the agent doesn't sell your script in that time, you have the option of terminating the agreement and seeking another agent. Ninety days is not a long time, and most people I know give their agents longer to perform. Skipping from agent to agent isn't usually productive. On the other hand, you don't want to give your agent too much time. After a while a script becomes stale and the agent is likely to lose enthusiasm for it. Once you sense that's happened, then it's time to leave.

If you're continuing to write and providing your agent with additional product, then you should see something happen within at least six months.

An agent isn't likely to pick you up as a client unless she firmly believes in both your talent and her ability to market you. Remember, you're not a milk cow; if your agent doesn't come up with anything for you, then your agent isn't coming up with anything for herself either. The investment is mutual; treat it with respect.

Chapter Ten

Inside the Hollywood Reader

Very few people understand what happens to a script after it is submitted, either through an agent or by the writer. Even experienced writers don't have a clue. I think it's willful ignorance: No one wants to know. Knowing would be too scary.

THE READER'S ROLE

The model of the reader comes from publishing. Editors prize their time, which is capitalized by ongoing projects and meetings with in- and out-of-house executives. Yet every day, rain or shine, manuscripts come cascading over the transom into the offices of the editor. Obviously an editor doesn't have the time to read every single manuscript that comes to her. So she relegates the responsibility to her assistant.

The editorial assistant—a euphemism for a reader—has to sort through the ton of pages sent in by agents and authors. The reader's responsibility is to sort through the pile and find those books that are worthy of further attention. Therefore the reader makes a determination: either send it out (in the mail and back to the author) or sent it up (to the producer or executive).

To send it back is easy. There's no risk in saying *no*. No one is standing over the reader's shoulder saying, "Are you sure you want to reject this? Maybe it's worth another look." For whatever reason, if the reader doesn't think the script should go up, then it goes out.

To say *yes* is a risk. If the work really is good and it becomes a book, you're a hero. But if the editor reads the book that you've recommended and then asks you what on earth you saw in it, your stock has just gone into a nose dive. As a reader, if you're going to say yes, you want to be sure your recommendation is going to be met with a positive response.

In Hollywood, studios, producers, directors—everyone—rely on readers, or, as they're sometimes known, story analysts. Some readers belong to the Screen Story Analysts Union, Local 854. (A union reader can make $46,000 a year reading seven and one-half scripts a week; more with overtime.) Other readers are freelancers who get paid by the script. (A freelancer usually makes anywhere from $30 to $50 per script and will typically read thirty scripts a week.) There are no formal requirements to become a reader. You don't need a college degree in English Literature. You don't even need a college degree. Anyone can be a reader, if they have a knack for recognizing dramatic structure.

COVERAGE

Let's say you have an "in" with a big-name producer and you manage to get the script to his or her office. Chances are your script will then go to a reader for what is called *coverage*.

Coverage is the reader's report about your script. It doesn't matter if you're a complete unknown or an industry giant: Your script will end up in the hands of a reader. Roger Simon, author of *The Big Fix*, *Scenes From a Mall* and *Enemies: A Love Story* resigns himself to the inevitable reader, but also tries to make sure the real decision-maker also looks at it. "That's called marshaling your clout and the clout of your allies," he says.

The format for coverage is fairly standard. It consists of three parts.

1. *The Synopsis*. The reader condenses your story into its main concept.

2. *The Analysis*. The reader describes what they believe are the strengths and weaknesses of your work.

3. *The "Box Score."* In a word, the reader makes an evaluation of your work. There are three options: *yes*, *no* or *maybe*. (Or in some circles, *recommend*, *pass*, *consider*.) Some coverages have an expanded *Box Score* which rate the story, characters, style and dialogue in terms of *good*, *fair* or *poor*.

The reader for a producer faces the same political complications as the reader for a book editor. To say *yes* is to take a risk, a risk few are willing to take. It's easier, and more importantly, it's safer for a reader to hedge his bets and say *maybe* than to go out on a limb and commit to a *yes*. That translates into the fact that instead of three potential responses to a script, there are only two: *maybe* and *no*.

"It doesn't stop at readers," says one reader for a studio. "Studio executives are always unwilling to get behind projects. The job of everybody up the ladder is to say *no*. Readers just reflect corporate reality."

That opinion is shared by studio executives. Michael Lansbury, the vice president of series programming for MCA Television Entertainment agrees: "Paranoia about going out on a limb runs all through studio ranks. It runs right up to vice presidents, senior vice presidents, executive vice presidents. Most executives will approach that limb very tentatively. Readers are the same way."

How does a reader know what to look for? There are no published guidelines, there's no list of films or ideas wanted. Does the reader simply rely on their own personal taste? Not if they want to stay employed. Readers develop a keen sense of what kind of material their boss likes. If they're working for a studio, then they also pay attention to what actors are under contract and what other projects are in production. Or if the reader works for an actor, they have a sense of what would work for that actor. The pieces have to fit. So if your script is rejected, it may have nothing to do with the quality of your story or your writing at all. It may be politics. As usual.

Still, some writers believe that being reviewed by an anonymous reader may be the lesser of two evils. If the head honcho had to read your script, it would probably be in a hurry and at the least opportune time: in the limo; in the bathroom; over a pastrami sandwich at Nate and Al's; or in bed just before lights out.

At least the reader is paid to pay attention to your work.

■ Chapter Eleven ■

Inside the Writers Guild

hroughout this book I make constant reference to the Writers Guild. Most writers who aren't members are aware of its existence but aren't sure what the Guild does other than register scripts and provide a list of sanctioned agents. The Guild plays a key role in the business life of the writer. You don't have to be a member of the Guild in order to benefit from the full range of its services, provided you are working for a signatory company; the Guild offers a variety of services to nonmembers, many of which have already been mentioned in this book. Don't undervalue the importance of the Guild; it champions the rights of writers at a very practical level.

WHAT THE GUILD DOES

The Guild is active in eight major areas. It would take too much space to explain each function in detail, so here is an outline:

1. *Contracts*
   a. Negotiation of basic agreements in screen, television (live, tape and film), radio and staff arrangements (newswriters).
   b. Administration of:
      1. Handling writer's claims
      2. Checking individual writers' contracts for Minimum Basic Agreement violations
      3. Enforcing working rules
      4. Processing grievances
      5. Arbitrating under the Basic Agreements
      6. Collecting and processing television and film residuals
      7. Pension plan
      8. Health and welfare plans

2. *Credits*
   a. Receiving of tentative notices
   b. Arbitrating protests
   c. Maintaining credit records
   d. Distributing credit manuals
   e. Providing credit information to members, producers, agents and companies
3. *Literary Material*
   a. Registration service
   b. Collaboration agreements
   c. Settlement of disputes

4. *Agents*
   a. Recording, filing and administering individual agreements between writers and agents
   b. Distributing lists of authorized agents
   c. Arbitrating disputes between writers and agents

5. *Employment*
   a. Compiling and distributing TV market lists
   b. Compiling and circulating film and television credits lists to producers and agents
   c. Compiling and circulating statistical data

6. *Information*
   a. Responding to inquiries by producers regarding member credits, agents, contract provisions and minimums
   b. Responding to inquiries by members and nonmembers regarding contract provisions

7. *Affiliation and Cooperation*
   a. Writers Guild of Great Britain
   b. Australian Writers Guild
   c. Writers Guild of Canada
   d. New Zealand Writers Guild
   e. Permanent Charities Committee

8. *Public Relations*
   a. Newsletter
   b. Trade press
   c. TV forums
   d. Annual awards event

9. *Instruction*
   a. Hosting workshops and seminars on a wide variety of writer's issues

WHAT THE GUILD DOES NOT DO

The Guild will not get you a job or recommend you for one. It doesn't act as an intermediary for production companies who want to hire writers.

HOW TO JOIN THE WRITERS GUILD OF AMERICA

The Guild won't accept you just because you've applied. You have to qualify for application by accumulating a certain number of writing units based upon a schedule that is published by the Guild (called Schedule of Units of Credit); the schedule determines the credit values for the work you do. You must total a minimum of twenty-four credits within three years based upon work completed under contract of employment or upon the sale or licensing of previously unpublished and unproduced literary or dramatic material. The employment must be with a company that is a signatory to the Writers Guild Collective Bargaining Agreement.

Once you qualify, then you can apply for membership (along with a cashier's check or money order for $2,500).

The Writers Guild is actually two separate guilds. One is in New York and the other is in Los Angeles. Writers who live east of the Mississippi River should apply to the New York Guild (WGAE), and writers who live west of the Mississippi should apply to the Los Angeles Guild (WGAW).

For more information contact the Writers Guild in your district:

Writers Guild of America, East
555 W. Fifty-seventh St.
New York, NY 10019
(212) 767-7800; FAX (212) 582-1909

Writers Guild of America, West
7000 W. Third St.
Los Angeles, CA 90048-4329
(213) 951-4000; FAX (213) 782-4802

NONMEMBER SERVICES

The Writers Guild offers important services to writers who aren't members, including:

1. Script registration service;
2. List of agents who have signed the WGA Artists' Manager Basic Agreement of 1976;
3. Information service (such as providing its members' agents' names);
4. The Television Market List, featuring contact submission information on current weekly prime-time television programs, published monthly in *The Journal of the Writer's Guild of America*. (Issues are available for $5 per issue or you may subscribe for $40 per year.)

SCHEDULE OF MINIMUMS

Every three years the Guild publishes a revised *Schedule of Minimums*. This schedule spells out in detail the theatrical and television basic financial agreements for work done by writers. If you don't belong to the Guild, these figures can act only as guidelines so you know what the going rate is for a particular job. This doesn't mean you're going to get the minimum amount stipulated by the Guild, but it does let you know what *minimums* the market is paying to Guild writers.

For example, for a flat deal for the purchase of an original screenplay (with the treatment), the writer should receive somewhere between $42,466 and $79,656 depending upon the budget of the film. The Guild also makes specific pay provisions for each step in the development and delivery of a creative work, including fees for rewrites and polishes.

Television is a lot more complicated for a writer than theatrical screenplays, and so most of the information in the schedule concerns television. (The theatrical schedule takes up only five pages; the television schedule takes up twenty-six.) The schedule covers many different categories from network prime time to documentary, news, and once-per-week non-dramatic programs.

To get your own copy—and you really shouldn't be without one—send two dollars to the Writers Guild and request one.

OTHER PUBLICATIONS YOU CAN GET

The Guild will also send you, for a small fee ($3.00), a pamphlet from its Writers Guild Series that addresses some of the issues of perpetual interest to writers. The three available pamphlets are:

- Creative Rights
- Plagiarism & Copyright Infringement
- Guidelines for Writers, Producers & Executives

For more information, you can request the:

- Agency List ($2.00 by mail with SASE)
- 1988 Minimum Basic Agreement ($18.00 by mail)
- 1995 Schedule of Minimums (free with Minimum Basic Agreement, or $2.00 by mail)
- Annual Directory of Members ($20.00 by mail)
- 1976 Artists Manager Agreement ($4.00)

The Writers Guild is a valuable resource for the writer even if you're not a member. *The Journal of the Writer's Guild of America, West* is especially helpful, not just for its Television Market List but for the wide variety of articles and interviews; I strongly recommend it.

Chapter Twelve

Inside the Deal

You've finished your script. The time has come for you to make a critical decision on how you want to get your screenplay read. Based upon what some of the people who were interviewed for this book have said, you may feel that you want to market your script yourself. Or, you may feel that the work is best left to an agent.

MARKETING YOUR OWN SCRIPT

You've decided to try to sell your own script. Maybe you have a friend who knows an A-list actor or director; maybe you know somebody who works in a production office somewhere. In any case, you think you have a shot at getting your script read by somebody who can make a decision. But, if you're going to act on your own behalf, you'd better know how to conduct an intelligent conversation with someone who may be interested in either optioning or buying your script.

First, a warning. It would be reckless for me to give you the idea that you could effectively negotiate a contract on your own behalf, and it would be foolish of you to think you could. Contracts are very complex.

The golden rule about contracts is simple: they're always written to favor the person who is presenting them, which is definitely not you. It takes years to learn the language and the ins and outs of contract negotiations. You need a professional to act on your behalf. So even if you're successful in finding a buyer for your work, you should enlist the help of an agent to draft the contract. *Representing yourself during contract negotiations is the single most grievous error you could make.*

Don't make the mistake of believing you're saving yourself the agent's 10 percent commission by doing the deal yourself. If you learn anything from this chapter, hopefully you will learn that the self-represented writer has a fool for a client. When negotiations start, turn them over to a professional. Finding an agent at this point is not hard.

Besides, a good agent won't cost you a penny.

How can I say that?

I've worked both ways as a writer: as a maverick without an agent and with an agent. I work without an agent only when I know and trust the people I'm working with, and that's *rare*. I have a long working relationship with a certain producer, and my fees have already been established. I like keeping my business relations with this producer uncomplicated, and it acts as an expression of trust on my part. It's paid off: My easy-going attitude has brought me steady work. But I definitely *don't* recommend taking this approach with people you don't know.

Having said that, I have no doubt, however, that if an agent had represented me all along, I would've gotten a better deal. Had I had an agent I might have negotiated a deal that would have not only covered the agent's 10 percent, but also brought some additional money back to me. When I say that a *good* agent won't cost you anything, it means that your agent will negotiate a better financial deal than you can, and by so doing, cover his or her commission and then some. A good agent is indispensable, even if you plan to market your own work.

On the other hand, you shouldn't be ignorant of the process of negotiating contracts. The more you know about how it works, the more you'll be able to contribute to the negotiation process rather than just shrugging your shoulders and saying, "You do whatever you think is best."

Let's go through the process of marketing your own script. There is no standard operating procedure—oftentimes it's little more than a shot in the dark—but certain things do tend to happen, and you should be aware of them. After warning you about not being your own agent, it may sound like I'm going against my own advice. Not really. You should feel free to initiate the process of finding the studio, independent producer or director who is interested in your work. Once you get the ball rolling and are ready to negotiate a contract, make sure you have an agent to represent your interests.

THE RELEASE

Most likely if someone agrees to read your script, he or she will want you to send a release *first*. If you want your script to be read, you have to read and return the release. Without it, your script will come back to you unread.

A typical release states that the reader shall not be held accountable in case you should sue them later for appropriating your idea. This may sound like a license to steal, but it really isn't. Rumors to the contrary, stealing is rare. It does happen, but think for a moment: Why would anyone want to steal an idea from you? As a beginning screenwriter, you're a downright bargain. The purchase price for your script is so low compared to the going rates of established screenwriters that it doesn't make sense to steal. Even if your script were atrocious, a producer would be more inclined to pay you $50,000 for the idea and have the script rewritten than to risk a lawsuit.

GRAND LARCENY

We are a litigious society. The remedy to any wrong in our society—real or perceived—is to sue. There is a pervasive, almost paranoid sense among writers, both beginning and established, that studio executives, producers, and sometimes even actors and directors will steal an idea at the drop of a hat. Dorothy Parker once said, "The only -ism Hollywood believes in is plagiarism."

The first question out of a writer's mouth invariably is, "How do I protect myself against having my idea stolen?"

I hear story after story from writers who claim that their idea has been stolen. It's even happened to me: I had an idea, submitted it only to have it rejected, and a year later a film was released with the exact same premise. How do you explain that? Does it confirm the suspicion that the industry is just helping itself to ideas submitted by unwitting writers?

Believe it or not, that fear is largely unmerited. The reason for these strange similarities has to do with a concept I call "the core fantasy."

The Core Fantasy

I've read more scripts over the past twenty years than most people in the industry. At any given time, I know what people are thinking about. I'm absolutely convinced that scripts reflect the hopes and fears of society. There's a kind of collective unconscious that writers share. The writers themselves are unaware of it, but when you read hundreds of scripts yearly, you find certain patterns of thought that are common. And these patterns reflect who and what we are at any given time. I call these patterns "the core fantasy."

I've watched the core fantasy change periodically over the past twenty years. Not surprisingly perhaps, the core fantasy for men has been distinctly different than the core fantasy for women.

The core fantasy for men is the same now as it was twenty years ago.

The heart of what men think and write about can be captured in one word. Not sex. Not money. The core fantasy for men is Power. Getting it, wielding it and keeping it.

The core fantasy for women, however, has changed several times in the past twenty years, and it's changed in large part as a result of a heightened gender consciousness and the feminist movement.

In the sixties, before the sexual revolution really took hold, many women tended to write story after story that went something like this:

Gloria, 30, a prisoner of her twelve-year marriage is a housewife with two children. Her husband Frank is demanding and abusive. No matter what Gloria does to please him—cooking elaborate meals, keeping the house spotless— Frank continues to abuse her, mentally and physically. The marriage is loveless, and Gloria knows Frank is having an affair, but she is afraid to confront him because a part of her couldn't abide losing him.

Just the same, Gloria dreams of escape, a life free from tyranny. She dreams of returning to college to finish the degree she'd started before she'd met Frank. She sometimes threatens to leave him, but each time she does, he pleads with her to stay. He promises to change, but never does. Gloria swallows her suffering for the sake of her children, perhaps, or for her belief that things will get better if she just tries harder.

It sounds ludicrous now, but I couldn't count the number of scripts I read with variations of this story. They were often sad and moving; they expressed very deep emotions: fear and longing, alienation, isolation, a need for fulfilling love.

The core fantasy for women changed in the seventies. The cast of characters was the same, and the motifs were the same—entrapment, unfulfillment, abuse—but now Gloria questions whether she should sacrifice herself on the altar of family. At some point in the story:

She loads up the car with all her possessions while Frank is at work but then stops at the end of the driveway, unable to continue into the street. Where would she go? How would she support herself and the children? She sits at the end of the driveway for hours, and then, realizing her defeat, she backs the car into the garage and unloads everything. Maybe things will get better if she just tries harder.

By the early eighties, the core fantasy for women took a dramatic turn. Gloria gained conviction. The terms of her marriage were no longer acceptable. Now, instead of trying to sneak away, Gloria confronts Frank. Frank admits his sins and begs Gloria to stay. He promises to change:

"I love you, I can't live without you," he cries.

"No," says Gloria, and she gathers her courage and moves ahead with her own life.

It is her first act of power. Now, in the nineties, women share the core fantasy of men: power. They write about the same subject, but they perceive and characterize it differently than men.

If you'd submitted a script about characters like Gloria and Frank, you would've been one of a hundred or a thousand people writing the same story. But you would've felt the story was uniquely yours, and if the story had been rejected, you might have seen something exactly like it on television six months later. Of course you'd think you'd been ripped off! The truth is, at any given time, somebody is thinking and feeling the same way you are. And that person may very well be writing a script.

This phenomenon is common even at the highest levels of thinking. Darwin is credited with developing the theory of evolution. But some say Alfred Russel Wallace actually came up with it first. Only he wasn't in a position to take credit for it. Who really invented the automobile or the airplane? Who was the true father of quantum physics? The answers are debatable. People in different countries were struck by the same ideas at the same time. History gives only one person the credit.

You can see this same phenomenon in films all the time. Why, suddenly, are there four different comic films about baseball? Why are there three films about medieval Scotland? Some years ago I was involved in a project about a bounty hunter. Early on we found out that someone else had written virtually the same script, and it became a race to production. The other guys won. (Why? Because Steve McQueen had attached himself to the project—it was his last film.) You might think that people hear about ideas and then steal them, but I don't think so. I think ideas spontaneously erupt in several places at the same time. So while you're writing your script, somebody somewhere else is probably writing the same script.

So you can see why everyone wants to protect themselves against getting sued. From your point of view it may look like you've been ripped off, but there's a good chance you weren't.

Stealing or Rewriting?

Well, you say, maybe they liked the idea but they didn't like the way the script expressed the idea, so they stole the idea and reshaped it. Probably not. It would be cheaper for the producer to buy your script and have it rewritten than to pay someone to start from scratch. Anyway, virtually every script that's written goes through rewrite. It doesn't matter if you're Shane Black or Joe Eszterhas or Babaloo Mandel, the script is going to go through a rewrite. (The only exception to this rule is if you have a rare exclusivity clause in your contract, which guarantees that you'll be the only writer on a project. Even that clause doesn't mean you won't have to rewrite your own script.)

A few years ago I was having lunch with a very successful writer-director, Colin Higgins, who had just finished directing *The Best Little Whorehouse in Texas*. Higgins was a master of comedy, authoring such films as *Harold and Maude*, *Silver Streak*, *Foul Play* and *Nine to Five*. I asked him about his coauthor on *Nine to Five*, Patricia Resnick. According to Higgins, the script was originally written and submitted by her. He thought the concept was brilliant, but he didn't like the way Resnick had constructed the story. He bought the script and rewrote it himself. Very little of Resnick's original script remained (although it would be interesting to get her version of the story). According to Writers Guild guidelines, you can't get a writing credit on a rewrite unless you've rewritten at least 51 percent of the script. I suppose Higgins could have stolen Resnick's idea and taken sole credit for the new script himself. But why open yourself up to almost certain litigation? It is both morally and financially prudent for a producer or director to buy the property and then make whatever adjustments are necessary to get the project off the ground.

I'm not going to say stealing doesn't happen, because it does. But usually only by reckless, fly-by-night people or studios. Established industry people tend to be cautious, if not for moral reasons then because they are fearful of being sued.

I have one story that is the writer's worst nightmare, and it illustrates the politics of filmmaking. A producer with whom I'd worked before telephoned me and asked if I was interested in doing a rewrite on an action script. I said, "Of course."

He sent me the script and we went over the kinds of changes he wanted. The story was basically solid, but it did need some work. "Time is short," he said. "How soon can you finish the rewrite?" (That same producer had once given me two weeks to write an adaptation from a novel—I did it in ten days—so he knew I could be fast if I had to be.)

I mumbled something and he said, "Fine, do it."

Two days later, he called back. "How are you doing on the rewrite?"

"Great," I said. (I hadn't even started yet.)

"Well, hold off," the producer said.

"What's the problem?"

"No problem. Just wait 'til I get back to you." He hung up.

I waited. Several days went by and he called again. "How's the rewrite coming?" he asked.

I reminded him that he'd told me to stop. "Oh, that," he said. "All taken care of. Get to work on it."

I thought it was a little bizarre, but it wasn't my place to question him, so I went back to thinking about the rewrite.

Then he called again.

"How's the rewrite coming?" he asked.

"It's coming."

"Good, good," he seemed pleased. "Listen, I want you to do something for me."

"What?" I asked.

"Throw out the script. Start over from scratch."

"What do you mean?"

"I mean take the original idea and write your own script."

"That's stealing. You'll get sued."

"I know, *but that's what insurance is for*."

I found out several weeks later what was really going on. The producer had no intention of stealing the author's idea. It turns out that the original writer thought he could act and wanted the role of the lead as a condition of sale. The producer knew this was impossible, and he tried to convince the writer to drop the demand, but he wouldn't. So he told the writer that if he didn't drop his demand to play the lead, he'd have the screenplay rewritten without him. The writer said, "Go ahead, and I'll sue you."

The producer smiled and said, "Be my guest."

The producer had enough experience with writers to know that writers don't want their ideas stolen and don't want to have to go to the trouble and expense of getting a lawyer and suing—a process that would certainly take years. The producer was banking on the fact that the writer would rather see his own name in the credits than someone else's. He was right. Within the week, the writer dropped his demand to play the lead.

The producer never intended to steal the idea. He was just using me as leverage.

So sign the release. But to protect yourself, make absolutely certain that your script has been registered with the Writers Guild of America *before* you send it in to be read.

HOW TO REGISTER YOUR SCRIPT

Even though the chances of having your script stolen are very small, you should still be prudent and register your script with the Writers Guild.

By registering your script with the Guild, you establish the completion date and the identity of your script, which is called a "literary property."

Registration provides evidence of the writer's claim to authorship of the literary property and the date of its completion. "A writer has certain rights under the law the moment the work is completed," writes the Guild. "It is therefore important that the date of completion be legally established." Registration legally establishes that, as of a certain date, this idea and script were yours.

Registering your script doesn't protect your title (but then neither does the United States Copyright Office).

You don't have to be a member of the Guild in order to register your script. The procedure is simple and inexpensive.

First, send a copy of your finished screenplay (8½″ × 11″) unbound and without staples or brads to:

> Writers Guild of America, West
> 7000 W. Third St.
> Los Angeles, CA 90048-4329
> (310) 550-1000

The Guild will then seal your script in a timed and dated Registration Envelope. They will send you an acknowledgment receipt which will read:

> REGISTERED WGAW NO._____

Put this number on the title page of your script to let readers know that it's been registered.

Besides scripts, you can also register television series formats, step outlines and story lines. Be sure to use your full legal name and not a pseudonym, initials, or familiar forms of proper names. You want to avoid any problems later if you need to recover the material you have on deposit.

Your material will be protected for five years. You may renew the registration for another five years for the then current fee. *If you don't renew, the Guild will destroy your script.* The fee should accompany your request to renew. To get the registration forms and a copy of the instructions, call the Guild at (310) 550-1000 (10 AM to noon and 2 PM to 5 PM, Monday through Friday). The cost is five dollars if you're a member of the Guild, and ten dollars if you're not. Make sure you send a check with your script when you register it.

Okay, you've signed the release and you've registered your script. What happens next?

You wait.

Don't give up your day job. Don't sit around days on end waiting for the phone to ring. Don't get impatient and don't ever get on the phone and bombard the person with worrisome questions like, "Did you get the script? Have you read it yet? Whadja think?" Sit tight and wait. Sometimes it's an agonizingly slow process, but wait.

If you don't hear anything in six weeks, then I'd call and remind someone that it's been a month and a half. They'll apologize and tell you how hectic it's been around the office lately, but, no, they haven't forgotten you, and they'll get back to you as soon as they can. A little nudge won't hurt. But constant harassment will earn you zero.

REJECTION

If the response comes in the mail, it's bad news. It'll probably be your script with a polite and vague note about how your work "just isn't for us at this time," and they'll wish you success with your work elsewhere. Very polite and very bloodless.

Rejection is always hard to take, but if you want to write for show business, then you'd better thicken your skin. As I mentioned in an earlier chapter, I used to collect my rejections. I made a game out of it. I wanted to see how many rejections I could get from all the different studios. I was up to more than *sixty* rejections before I got my first real acceptance. I then threw away all my rejection slips and never looked back.

You can learn from your rejections, and you'd be foolish not to pay attention to what they're saying either outright or between the lines. There are all sorts of rejection letters, some better than others. Here are three basic letters and how to deal with them:

The Impersonal Rejection Letter

The worst rejection is the anonymous printed form letter. You never seem to take on the status of human being in the reader's eyes. The letter is perfunctory and soulless; there may not even be a signature.

With this type of letter, you don't learn much. If you aren't practiced in the art of rejection, you might make the mistake of taking the rejection personally and draw all kinds of wrong conclusions. One thing I learned a long time ago is that you can't guess the intent of the letter writer. The rejection may have absolutely nothing to do with the quality of your script or your skill as a writer. They don't tell you why you were rejected, and you don't know. Don't torture yourself with thoughts like, "Maybe I shouldn't write. Maybe I should join the foreign service."

If this kind of rejection serves any purpose, it is to test your resolve to become a writer. If you're easily dissuaded and give up after a rejection or two, then you didn't really want to write in the first place. But if you're still plugging away after ten, twenty, fifty rejections, then you're dedicated to the task.

Every once in a blue moon you may get a really nasty note. "It's people like you who give screenwriting a bad name. Give it up." This response is just mean-spirited. Ignore those comments. Don't take them to heart—unless you're looking for an excuse to quit.

The Personalized Rejection Letter

This type of rejection is the "very good, but . . ." letter, and in some ways it's the hardest to accept. You have a letter from a real human being with a name who is communicating directly with you. "We read your script and enjoyed it very much, but we found it lacked the type of structure we felt it needed to sustain two hours." Or, "We liked your writing and your obvious knack for plot, but we found your characters flat and uninteresting."

The good news is that they're taking the time to give you some genuine feedback. Their level of enthusiasm is usually indicated by the amount of time and energy they spend giving you a response. If it's a couple of lines, then they're only being polite and want to avoid giving you a form letter. (Don't underestimate the politeness, however; they are leaving the door open for you to come back.) If they go on at length, however, then you really have piqued their interest. Still, it's a rejection. My experience has been that rewriting the script to please the criticism never works. Still, receiving a letter like this is a confidence builder. You're on the right track; you're making headway.

The "What Else Do You Have?" Rejection Letter

If you have to be rejected, then this one isn't bad. "We didn't feel your script was right for us, but we were impressed with your ability to write. Do you have any other screenplays or treatments that we could look at?" This letter speaks for itself. But it can cause no end of grief if you're a one-script writer.

I recommend to all beginning writers that you write at least three and preferably five scripts for precisely this reason. One script may only serve to generate interest, and if you have nothing to fall back on, then you've lost a major opportunity. (Agents prefer clients who have more than one script too, because you're a lot easier to market with five stories than just one.) It's called having a body of work. Mix it up. Write a drama or two. Try a romantic comedy. So when the time comes and someone says, "What else do you have?" you won't get this pained expression on your face.

THE INSIDE PITCH

A common response to a well written script is a request for other ideas. The time may come when you have to actually pitch an idea to an executive. *Pitching* is an art form. Some people are absolutely brilliant at it; others dread the prospect of getting up in front of other people and outlining an idea for a film or a show.

Your future hinges on a couple of minutes and your ability to tease, enchant and convince. These skills aren't writerly skills. Most writers I know are boring people. They tend to be quiet, introspective and self-effacing. But when you pitch, you need to be dynamic, immodest and gregarious. It *is* a sales job, make no mistake about it. In the moments you pitch, you're no different than a vacuum salesman at the front door, and you'd better have a good opening line or you'll never get your foot in the door.

Before you practice your pitch, put yourself into the exec's shoes. Nobody knows how many pitches are made in any given week in Holly-wood, but the estimates are staggering. Pitching is a way of life for many freelance writers of episodic shows: You have to come in armed with two, three, five or more ideas at a time. Networks are barraged with pitches for new series. (One estimate: Each network hears about twenty pitches *a week*. That's over 1,000 pitches a year to each network.) Studios also listen to somewhere between twenty and thirty pitches a week. The number racks up: There's a pitch being thrown in every bar, restaurant, sauna, gym, office and bedroom in town. And then you get your invitation to make your pitch.

"Tell me whatcha got," says the exec.

The first time I made a pitch I felt like I'd just stood up in front of my fifth-grade class to recite something I'd memorized. The back of my neck started itching; my scalp crawled. "What am I doing here?" I asked myself. The exec looked mildly amused, as if he was enjoying my discomfort. I had two minutes to convince this man that my idea was worth millions of his dollars. That sounded so preposterous to me that I felt I was the punchline of some huge joke. I bumbled through my presentation, and when I was finished, even I wouldn't have given ten cents for my idea. The exec nodded and then knocked the ash off the end of his cigar. "Sounds interesting," he said. "It has potential." He looked at his assistant and then asked him, "What do you think, Jeff?"

Jeff said, "Sure, it has potential."

"You got anything else?" asked the exec.

Fortunately, I did.

Experience is a great teacher. I learned a great many things in that meeting, and if its only purpose was to serve as my education, then it was worthwhile. I now pass this wisdom along to you:

1. Above all, keep it brief. Everybody has a short attention span. Keep it simple, don't overcomplicate the pitch with subplots or layers of characterization.

2. Pretend you're talking to a group of third graders, not to your teacher. Don't use long sentences or try to express complex concepts. Don't use words with more than three syllables. Keep your vocabulary simple.

3. Develop a staccato rhythm. A slow, methodical presentation, no matter how well thought out, fails.

4. Get excited. Excitement is contagious.

5. Move around. Don't just sit in your chair like a corpse. Their eyes will be less likely to close if they have something to watch.

6. Use body language. Punctuate your presentation with your arms, your hands, your feet if you have to.

7. Always stay the center of attention. You are the focus; if you lose that, then you've lost control.

8. Don't let interruptions unnerve you. The phone rings, somebody comes in with an urgent question or message, or even the exec interrupts you with "Sorry, but I need to take care of this right now," and boom, there you are in mid-stride with no place to go. Distractions are inevitable, so be prepared to pick up where you left off. Don't let the interruptions irritate you; it'll reflect in your manner, and then your pitch will go sour.

9. Never repeat yourself. When you're finished, sit down and give the exec that "Well, whaddya think?" look.

10. Never, ever read your pitch. If you want to keep some notes to remind you of the key points you want to cover, fine, but use them only when your mind suddenly goes blank.

11. Never go in unrehearsed. The pitch that works in your head may not work out loud with other people, so find a willing victim and pitch to him or her. You'll learn what's working and what isn't when you have an audience.

To develop a good pitch, you have to combine equal parts of salesmanship with showmanship. You have to be entertaining and you have to capture the imagination of your audience. These skills don't come easily, but they do come with practice. So when the exec asks, "Watcha got?" you'll have an answer.

YES!

In this case, good news travels fast. If someone is interested in your script, they're not likely to write you a letter. They're going to call you.

Who wouldn't want to get a phone call from a production company, maybe from Dusty Hoffman or Sly Stallone, speaking directly to you, saying, "I read your script. It's great. I want to do it." This is the highest of highs for a screenwriter. In some ways it's a better high than actually seeing the film completed and in the theaters. Why? Because this comes out of the blue.

I was outside feeding my horse one day, when my wife shouted to me through the window that I had a phone call. "Take a message," I yelled back.

"You may want to take the call," she warned. "It's Charlton Heston."

I took the call.

No, he wasn't calling to tell me he'd read a script of mine and wanted to play the lead role, but phone calls like that do bushwhack you. You aren't prepared to talk intelligently. "I need some time to think this through!" your mind is screaming. But there's no time to gather your wits.

I know a writer who was called successively by Robert Redford, Dustin Hoffman, Alan Parker and Sherry Lansing. Each of them wanted a story of his. This was early in his career and he was downright stunned. Redford invited him to come down to visit him on location, which, of course, he did. He said he knew this was going to be a unique experience when he walked into the director's bungalow and the screen door was propped open with an Oscar (which Redford had recently won for *Ordinary People*). They shook hands and the writer said, "Glad to meet you, Mr. Redford."

"Call me Bob," Redford insisted. "Just plain Bob."

"Yeah," the writer thought, remembering the Oscar propping open the door. "Ordinary Bob."

That was no ordinary experience for him. Suddenly, he had something that Robert Redford wanted. How often does that happen? (By the way, Redford didn't get the project.)

So be prepared if someone calls with great news and then starts to ask some tough questions. Don't have this conversation:

Famous actor/director: "What do you want for a one-year renewable?"

You: "I dunno. Whatever you think is fair."

Dumb answer. Chances are you don't even know what a one-year renewable is. But you're so happy right now you'd take a dime if it was offered. Remember, the other person has the advantage. *Don't commit yourself to anything*, except to talk further.

Rather, have this conversation:

Famous actor/director: "What do you want for a one-year renewable?"

You: "Listen, I'm so happy right now I can't make any kind of decision on the spur of the moment. Can I think this through and talk it over with my agent? I'm sure we can work something out."

A ONE-YEAR RENEWABLE WHAT?

Your next call is to your agent. Don't have one? Get one *now*. Getting an agent is easy if you tell them that you've got a famous director/actor interested in your script. *Don't* get an agent that belongs to the same agency as the director/actor. Ask first! Then stand back and let the negotiations begin.

But keep yourself in the loop.

To keep yourself in the loop you need to know the basic sense of what your agent is haggling over with the producer. After all, you're the one who's got to do the work. The document in which all the details are laid out is called the option/purchase agreement.

The Option/Purchase Agreement

Don't be surprised when you find out that the producer doesn't want to buy your screenplay; rather, he wants to lease it. This procedure is normal. The lease is called an option. In effect, the option says that in return for a certain amount of money the producer can "lock in" the property while he or she goes out and tries to put together the people and financing for the picture. Once you sign an option, you are legally obligated to sell your script (called the "property") to that producer any time within the stipulated time frame of the option—usually a year, but maybe as short as six months.

If Steven Spielberg were to get wind of your optioned script and decide he wanted to make you an offer—even if the offer was equivalent to the annual gross domestic product of a small African nation—you're legally obligated to turn him down.

An option may be renewed at the pleasure of both parties, although your first option may have a clause in it that automatically guarantees another year option if the producer chooses to renew it. If the producer does choose to renew, he or she will have to pay another stipulated fee.

An option doesn't give the producer the right to make your film. It only gives him the right to *buy* it. In producer's parlance, this is called "controlling the rights."

Writers are always tempted by options, because it is a solid expression of interest in their work and because it is the first step towards getting a film made. But there are some dangerous pitfalls here.

The worst pitfall is the time factor. There are producers who love to option material and then just sit on the options. They make no effort to convert the option into a purchase.

Why do they do this? I don't really know. There's a certain major director-actor who has a terrible reputation for optioning scripts and story ideas and then sitting on them for years. In the case of one film that I know, it took him eight years to move from the option to the production. The film was adapted from a book, and after eight years, all the glow of what was then a best-selling book had long since faded. The writer was powerless. Of course he got his option check on the anniversary of each renewal.

You might ask yourself how can producers afford to keep paying out option money year after year? Simple. It's chump change. Ten thousand dollars a year for an option isn't a lot for some people. I've even heard a story of a producer-actor who options properties for the sole purpose of keeping them away from his rivals.

The basic concept of a option/purchase contract is pretty simple. The money the producer gives you for the option (let's say it's $10,000, the actual price depends upon a lot of factors which are covered later in this chapter) is a nonrefundable downpayment against the total purchase price of the script. Your agreement will outline how much money you expect to receive if the producer does buy the full rights to your screenplay.

Let's say your agent has negotiated a figure of $125,000 for the outright sale of your script, and a one-year renewable option for $10,000. That means the producer has one year to pay you an additional $115,000 in order to own the rights of your film. The $10,000 advance is deducted from the total amount of the purchase price.

The amount of the option is based loosely on the concept that you should receive 10 percent per year of the total value of the script. If you determine in your agreement that you'll sell your screenplay to the producer for $100,000 once they get the financing, then you should be entitled to roughly a $10,000 annual option payment. The figure, like all figures in this industry, is negotiable. But use this as a guideline.

Let's say that after one year the producer hasn't been able to put the package together, but he wants to renew the option agreement with you for another $10,000. You have the right of either saying "yes," in which case you'll get another check for $10,000 (which is *not* deducted from the total amount of the purchase price) or you can tell the producer to take a hike. If you don't renew, you now control the rights to your work and are free to market your script anywhere you want. Obviously a producer won't buy your script until he's reasonably certain that the project has a good chance of going ahead. Whether or not the producer is successful often has to do with things that have nothing to do with your script, so if the deal does collapse, it doesn't reflect on you. And you get to keep the option money as a consolation prize.

Let me dispel the impression that an option is always worth ten percent of the sales price. It may be worth that, or it may be worth $5,000 or $1,000 or even $1.

You say, what kind of yahoo would lock up a property for a year in return for a lousy buck?

You might.

Why?

It's called a *free option*, and they're not that unusual. If you believe in the producer—and that producer has the credentials and/or contacts that show an ability to deliver—and if the producer is willing to buy your screenplay for more money than you would've gotten if you'd received a bigger option payment, you might want to think about it.

Personally I wouldn't advise it, but I know others who disagree. It is a sad, but true, fact that once someone has a financial investment in your property, they are likely to work harder and longer to realize the project. If the producer doesn't have any earnest money invested, then all they lose is some time. Meanwhile, your script has been tied up for one or two years, with nothing to show for it. But you will have to judge the situation for yourself and decide whether the producer's sincerity, commitment and track record warrant giving up control of your rights.

An option/purchase agreement can be as simple as a memo and as complicated as a full-blown contract. Its complexity is over most of our heads, so you can see why it's best left to a professional agent.

CONTRACT CLAUSES

There are different types of contract clauses that may be included in your option/purchase agreement that are always negotiable and that you should know about.

Some sample clauses are:

THE EXCLUSIVITY CLAUSE. For writers, this clause is the brass ring on the contract carousel. It obligates the producer to make certain that you are the *only* writer for the project, including all rewrites. Maybe 2 percent of screenwriters are powerful enough to land this clause in their contract.

THE REWRITE CLAUSE. Your contract will guarantee you a certain number of rewrites before the producer can bring in a rewriter. The more rewrites you get included, the less likely a rewriter will be brought in. This clause also spells out how much money you get for each rewrite you do. It's standard policy for the producer to get at least one major rewrite and one minor rewrite (sometimes called "a polish") as part of the original fee. But if your agent negotiates three rewrites, then you will be paid an amount that is stipulated in the purchase agreement for each of the two additional rewrites.

This clause doesn't guarantee you either the work or the additional money. If the producer doesn't want or need additional rewrites, then you obviously won't get paid for doing them. (But you may qualify for a *bonus*.)

If the producer sours on you, then the producer may call in a rewriter even though you haven't done all three rewrites. If the producer does that, then he or she must pay you for the work you didn't do. In other words, the producer must pay you for the rewrites even though you didn't write them because they are now using a rewriter.

THE BONUS CLAUSE. Your script was written so well that the producer and/or the director felt it needed only a polish. So you do the polish and the writing is so good you wow them. "This is it," announces the producer, "the final draft."

"Well," you say, invoking your bonus clause, "how about showing a little appreciation?" After all you saved the production team precious time and money, the two most valuable commodities there are in filmmaking.

The writer may receive a bonus now or at any of a number of different times. There are four critical stages in the development of a film. You may be entitled to a bonus at the completion of one or all of these phases. Each phase is a critical milestone in the process, and to reach it represents a major accomplishment. The four stages are:

1. Delivery of a finished script
2. The start of production
3. The end of production
4. The release of the film

Before a film starts production, it is in "development." Most scripts never get out of development. That's why it has the nickname "development hell." People have big plans, but reality has a nasty habit of intruding, and what seems like a sure thing withers on the vine. The step from preproduction to production is the biggest step, and if you can survive that transition, then each step becomes easier.

Bonuses recognize the importance of these milestones.

You may receive a bonus at any one or all of the production steps. Bonuses are not automatically part of an option/purchase agreement.

THE FIRST RIGHT OF REFUSAL CLAUSE. Writers sometimes get stuck in the "now." They need also to look ahead. What if your script becomes a hit movie? In an industry that loves sequels, you may want the right to write the sequel(s). This clause gives you the right to do that. You don't have to do it if you don't want, but at least you have the right to make up your mind.

THE POINTS CLAUSE. Otherwise known as the "carrot or the stick" clause. During negotiations the producer sweetens the pot by offering you a percentage of net profits. The usual range is from two to five percent. A point is one percent; five points are five percent.

The key word here is "net." Net means after all expenses are paid. If you have a deal that entitles you to three points of net, then you will collect 3 percent of the film's profits.

Producers may try to lure the writer into taking a lower salary for a higher percentage of the net profits. This is known as a deferral.

Let me be emphatic about this point. If I had a choice of taking $50,000 (the Guild minimum) for writing a script with no participation in the net profits and $25,000 with 50 percent of the net profits, I'd take the $50,000.

Net points are also called *monkey points*. I'm not sure why, but I think it's because you'd have to have the mind of a monkey to accept them. You'll almost never see nickel one from your profit participation, even if you had a share of a mega-blockbuster movie.

How can that be?

Two reasons. First, over 90 percent of movies made today lose money. That shouldn't be startling because the same is true in the publishing industry. Most books that are published lose money. But the movies and books that do make money, make so much of it that they cover all the other losses and still turn a healthy profit for the studios. So to start, your film has less than one chance in ten to make a profit.

Second, the studios are in charge of the bookkeeping. Mario Puzo, author of both the book and the screenplay *The Godfather*, once told me that he never made a single dime on his points in the picture because Paramount said the film was still in the red years after its release. Winston Groom had net points in *Forrest Gump* and didn't see a nickel either, and yet it is rumored that Tom Hanks made over $30 million from his profit participation. Why did Hanks make so much money and Groom none? Because Hanks had gross points (based on box office sales) and Groom had net points (based on studio bookkeeping). I don't think there's a person on this planet, with the exclusion of the accounting department at Paramount, who believes *The Godfather* lost money. A lot of it. That's no solace to Mario Puzo. (Don't feel too badly for Winston Groom: he sold the sequel to *Gump* for a reported $4 million.)

There are reasons why such a great disparity is possible.

If Tom Hanks got $30 million for his share of gross profit, then that money had to be charged against production costs of the film. And what about the producers and the director? How many gross points did they have? How many additional millions of dollars had to be charged against production? All these people have to be satisfied before you move over to calculate net points.

The second reason is just as compelling. If the production budget of a movie is $100 million, then you would expect profit to begin at $100,000,000.01. Not so. Profit begins at something like $400 million! I've heard various figures from producers and directors, but the range for breaking even is somewhere between 3.8 and 4.1 *times* the production cost! That would cover all the marketing, advertising, theater commissions, gross point participations, distribution costs, *ad infinitum, ad nauseam.* How many films do you know that have made more than $400 million? Precious few. You can count them on one hand. When it comes to getting on the gravy train, the writer with net points is way at the end of the line. He'll be lucky if he gets to lick the empty bowl.

Net points? Forget 'em.

There are those, including agents, who would disagree, but I've yet to hear a persuasive argument. *Always get as much money as you can up front.* Don't let anyone tempt you with sugary dreams of buckets of dough on the other end. There isn't another end, not for writers.

There are exceptions, of course. You may be involved in a small budget, independent picture, and you're more interested in getting the movie made than in how much money you're going to get. The producer may ask you to defer part or all of your fee in order to get the film done. Fine. If you believe in the film, and you believe in the people who are making the film, and you want to see it done at any cost, then don't let questions of money get in the way. But understand: in all probability you're not deferring your salary, you're giving it up. Chances are you'll never see anything more than what you got up front. And make sure you ask the producer who else is deferring their fees. Is he? Are the actors? The DP? And so on. If you're satisfied that everyone is taking an equal cut in order to make the film go, then it may be a reasonable decision. But if you've been singled out to make the sacrifice, I'd say it was time to do some straight talking.

ADDITIONAL CLAUSES. You may have other clauses in your option/purchase agreement that have to do with collateral income. Let's say your movie spawns clothing (t-shirts, caps, sweatshirts, pajamas) or toys or spinoff books (including comics) or hot and cold drink tumblers. It's a big world out there and thousands of people are ready to merchandize their products with movie logos on them. The mind boggles at the possibilities: sheets, beach towels, lunch boxes, there was even "Great Gatsby" scotch when the movie came out. You should get a portion of these profits. Don't scoff at the possibility. Clever merchandizing has netted some writers more money than they made for their screenplay.

There is no standard form for an option/purchase agreement. Depending on what terms you reach with your agent and with the producer, you may complete what's called an option/purchase memo. The memo is short, and in essence, what it does is *agree to agree* to work out all the details of the agreement at a later date. Producing an option/

purchase agreement takes hours of legal time, and at $200 or more per hour, some people would rather avoid big legal charges up front. When the producer knows for sure that the film is going to fly, then they'll hammer out the details with you. It's a good faith agreement, which means that both parties will be reasonable when the time comes to polish off the details. Does it matter if you sign a memo versus a full agreement? Not really. What matters is that if the project goes forward, out of option and into production, that every detail is spelled out clearly and unambiguously.

WHAT'S A SCREENPLAY WORTH THESE DAYS?

The simplest answer is that a screenplay is worth a lot. The Writers Guild publishes minimums that a writer who belongs to the Guild should be paid for different categories of writing. How much you get paid depends on all kinds of factors, such as whether your script is for television or a theatrical release; whether it is a flat deal; whether the budget is small, medium, or large; and so forth. A committee at WGA sets these standards, and they are revised every three years.

If you're not a member of the Writers Guild, then there are no minimums, but the WGA's standards are used as guidelines pretty much everywhere. For example, a low-budget film (which is a film with a below-the-line budget of less than $2.5 million) would pay the writer a minimum of $39,452 for a screenplay and a treatment. An extra rewrite is worth $12,946, and a polish is worth $6,476. Remember, these are minimums for a low-budget film.

The minimums for a high-budget film (which is defined as a film with a below-the-line budget of more than $2.5 million) are very different. The minimum for a screenplay and treatment in this case is $74,002. A rewrite is worth $19,736, and a polish is worth $9,867.

The WGA also provides fee schedules for original stories, treatments and various drafts. It even stipulates how much money should be paid in each installment. If a producer agrees to pay you the minimum of $39,452 for a treatment, first draft and final draft, then the Guild dictates that you should be paid $17,877 on delivery of the treatment; $15,538 on delivery of the first draft, and $6,037 on delivery of the final draft. (These figures change constantly, and so chances are that as you read this they are higher. Contact the Writers Guild for the most recent minimums.)

Remember, these are *starting* points. You can negotiate upwards from them.

A former student of mine is a very talented writer. He shopped a screenplay while he was still in film school, and a well-known production house liked it, wanted it, and was willing to sign an agreement. But all they offered him was $8,000 for his screenplay, plus another $6,000 for a rewrite. The offer was outrageous, but if you've never sold a screenplay before and you see a chance to break into the majors, would you sell it for $14,000? You might say, "Hey, it's $14,000 I didn't have yesterday." You hear these rationalizations every day. "Once I get a couple of credits, then I can ask for bigger money." But, he turned down the offer, even though he needed the money badly. He wasn't going to give his screenplay away, which is what he would've been doing if he'd signed the deal. He's since gone on to write several other screenplays, one of which is about to enter production with a major star. He held out, and it was rough going for a while, but he's going to make it.

Years ago a literary agent named Scott Meredith did something that other agents at the time thought was immoral. Representing a writer, he sent copies of the manuscript around to different publishing houses and told the editors that if they were interested in the property, then they had until noon the following day to make a bid. The approach was unheard of. Prior to Meredith, an author submitted his or her manuscript to one house at a time. If the house was interested, it made an offer. If the house wasn't interested, it politely declined. To make what is called "multiple submissions" was considered unethical. For whom? Not the writer. The advantage clearly belonged to the publishing house. It could take its time without fear of competition.

Scott Meredith blew a hole in the practice. Cursing Meredith, the editors scrambled to make bids. The result was a record-breaking offer for the author. The advantage now belongs to the author.

Today Meredith's approach is a standard technique. The agent who believes that your work is strong enough and has enough commercial appeal will put your script out to bid and hope that the studio execs will claw their way to the top of the heap. If a bidding war starts on your script, forget all about minimums. You could easily go past the one-million-dollar mark.

Now you have an idea of some of the twists and turns involved in contract negotiations. If, after all this, you still don't think you need an agent, then you either have a brilliant business mind or you have delusions of grandeur. And we haven't even talked about the development deal yet.

THE ADVANCED COURSE

Congratulations, you've gotten past elementary contracts. If you're either totally disgusted and/or thoroughly confused, and you don't want anything more to do with the business end of the movie business, you can skip the rest of this chapter. If, on the other hand, you're fascinated with all the details of making a deal, then we'll get into the meat of it.

The Step Deal

The step deal, often called the development deal, is the heart of contracts. Option/purchase agreements are far less common.

In this scenario, you're a hired gun.

"Who's going to hire me?" you ask.

Let's say you write a script. Your agent shops it around. A producer, director or studio exec reads it but doesn't think the story's right. But you impressed her with your writing talent. "This person knows how to tell a story. This person knows how to develop character," the exec thinks. So, instead of buying your script, the exec offers you a development deal.

The development deal is a collaboration between the producer and the writer, except that the writer works at the producer's discretion; in other words, you're an employee. The fact that you're working for a producer doesn't mean you punch a clock or are paid by the hour. But you are paid to do a job.

For every feature film that gets produced, there are probably at least ten development deals in the works. (Some calculate the figure at twice that.) Using the more conservative figure of 1:10, means you have *ten times* the chance of writing a script as part of a development deal than you have of selling a script outright. This increases your odds dramatically of getting work as a screenwriter.

A step deal (which is a type of development deal) takes the writer stage by stage through the scriptwriting process. The deal protects the producer more than it protects the writer because it forces a review of your work at each stage.

THE FIRST STAGE. The exec may ask you if you have any story ideas. Or he may ask you to develop one of his or her own ideas. Or it may be a combination of both. If a producer wants to develop your idea, you'll be paid additional compensation for it in the form of an option, similar to the kind of option you read about in the previous chapter. This option guarantees the producer exclusive rights to your story for the time stipulated in the option, typically a year. You get to keep the option money whether or not the film gets made.

Based upon your idea or an idea suggested by the producer, you then have to write a *treatment*, which is a narrative summary of the fleshed-out story.

There are two types of treatments: the short treatment (sometimes called a rough treatment, which typically runs between five and ten pages) and the long treatment (sometimes called a full treatment, which is a scene-by-scene narrative and may run thirty-five pages).

Upon delivery of the treatment, the producer will then decide if you should continue to the next step.

THE SECOND STAGE. The producer likes your treatment. It has a lot of promise, and he wants to see it developed. He may have suggestions for change, which you are obligated to include, unless you can argue that those inclusions would hurt the story. The producer has given you the green light: Now your job is to convert the treatment into a full script.

My experience has been that producers can sometimes be cavalier about their ideas. They don't always think them out clearly, and so it falls upon you to protect the story from ideas that come out of left field. But if the producer insists, you have only two options: either include the ideas or quit.

One producer used to send me clippings of stories from the pages of *The New York Times*. Even stretching my imagination, they had nothing to do with the story I was writing for him. It was up to me to tell him that including a subplot about Jewish diamond merchants who were getting robbed in New York City had no place in a story set in West Virginia during the Depression. "Well," he said wistfully, "you never know." He never stopped sending me clippings.

THE THIRD STAGE. You submit your script to the producer. He reads it. If you've done a terrible job, he can terminate your employment. (But you still have to be paid for the work you did up to that point. See the section below.) If you've done a good job, then you get to move to the third and final stage, the rewrite.

Based on story conferences with the producer, you may be asked to make major or minor changes in the screenplay. You may not like the suggestions, and you should argue according to what you believe is the artistic integrity of the story, but—and this is a major but—it's the producer's screenplay and he can do whatever he wants. It would be a major mistake for you to get too proprietary about the screenplay. You're a writer for hire, and as such, you are in the service of another.

Remember, you can quit.

Your particular contract may call for a specific number of rewrites. Probably one or two. If the producer wants additional rewrites that aren't included in your original contract, then you should be paid extra for them.

Which brings up the issue of money.

GETTING PAID. Let's start with the bad news first.

Don't expect the same kind of money you'd get from an outright sale. You may get anywhere from 25 to 50 percent of the money you might have gotten if you'd sold it directly depending upon whether you're writing for the screen or for television. The script that was worth $100,000 in a sale might only generate $25,000 to $50,000 in a step deal. You'd get a third of the money upon the completion of the treatment, a third when you handed in the completed script, and the final third when you finished the rewrite(s). (This assumes, of course, that you've been employed through the entire process. The producer has the right to drop you at the completion of any step and bring in another writer if he so desires.)

The good news balances out the bad and then some.

First, remember, you have ten to twenty times the chance of getting a development deal than of selling a spec script outright.

Second, the bonuses are terrific. If your script *does* go to production, then you should receive a bonus that will bring up the total to at least what you would've made with an outright sale and perhaps more. This bonus doesn't depend on the whim of a producer; rather, it is guaranteed in your agreement. The downside of this is that less than 10 percent of films in development ever get out of development and onto the screen.

If you get a $30,000 fee for your step deal, and the project goes forward to production, you might get a bonus of $80,000. Remember, these figures are low, and you're likely to be negotiating for substantially more. That's why you have an agent, remember?

A step deal is a crapshoot for both the producer and the writer. As a writer, you may or may not get to go the distance, but at least you can take solace in the knowledge that you'll be paid each step of the way.

TURNAROUND. There's one more rub you should know about called a *turnaround*.

Let's say a producer hired you to write a script, which you did brilliantly. But the producer couldn't find a studio or the money to back the project. Not your fault.

Under the normal terms of a step deal, since the producer hires you to write the script for him, he owns the rights to the script, whether produced or not. If the story was yours, the rights to the story revert to you once the option expires. At that point you're free to sell your story again. But you can't sell the script, because it belongs to the producer.

Unless—and this is an interesting exception—you find someone else who has connections and access to the money to make the film. The original producer *is obliged to sell the property* to this person in return for any and all his expenses, such as your fees and all the verifiable costs of doing business. In other words, a dead deal doesn't have to stay dead.

The turnaround fee is always negotiable. The failed producer would rather recoup a portion of his expenses than lose it all.

Turnaround scripts are quite common in the industry. It's been estimated that as many as a quarter of all the scripts that go into production in Hollywood are in turnaround.

Chapter Thirteen

Inside Television

T elevision writers are the most scorned, the best paid, and in some respects, the most underrated writers around today. They are scorned within the film industry as hacks—formula writers who cater to the base tastes of the mindless television masses. Some of the writers themselves will confide in a reflective moment that they feel like they've sold out. Other writers are adamant about their skills and feel that writing for television flexes more muscles than writing for the screen. In addition, the work is steady. Whereas a successful screenwriter does a film every two or three years, a television writer has to produce twenty-six prime time shows a year, and a soap writer has to crank out about 260 shows a year! The pressure is unrelenting, and it takes a special kind of person to work under those conditions.

Television is a factory. It survives on an endless stream of product: half-hours, hours, and mini-series. With the proliferation of cable channels, the demand for product has increased dramatically in the last ten years. And the demand continues to rocket skyward. That's the good news; the bad news is that as more and more channels vie for a relatively flat base of viewers, budgets shrink. More shows; smaller budgets.

Network television is no longer king. An increasing number of channels have gone into production: HBO, USA, TBS, Showtime and the Sci-Fi Channel have all produced original dramas. Even the Discovery Channel, long a bastion of nonfiction, documentary films, has announced plans to produce feature works. Many writers overlook the possibility of working for network television or DBS (Direct Broadcast Satellite) because of the stigma of writing for the tube. It is a silly and self-defeating attitude.

HOW TO DO IT

The procedure of pitching and writing for television is as complicated as it is varied. There is no standardization. Each outfit has its own way of doing things. If you're interested in writing for a particular show, then you will need to do some homework in order to make a professional presentation.

As an example, I've chosen a popular, independent syndicated series that most people are familiar with: *Star Trek: Deep Space Nine*. Because information and procedures constantly change, you shouldn't accept this information as current or accurate. I'm using it as an example of what you need to know and what obstacles you might encounter when trying to write for a television program.

Popular shows like *Deep Space Nine* attract a lot of attention. My advice to beginning writers has always been not to try to break in with the top-ten Nielson-rated shows. They don't need help; they're doing fine without you. Look at the middle and at the bottom of the Nielsons: Those shows are in trouble. Those shows need help; they need good scripts. A show in the middle third of the rankings wants to rise; it may be hungry for good writers. A show in the bottom is probably desperate for good writers.

But a word of caution. To write well for a show, you have to know and believe in the show. You have to be a fan. If you have any contempt for the show or its premise then that attitude will be reflected in your work. You may accidentally end up writing a parody of the show. So before you decide to write, watch several episodes, study them, dissect them, try to figure out what's going wrong and how it might be fixed. You can't do radical surgery (i.e. introduce new characters, change the premise, etc.) but a good script is a life preserver for a sinking show.

Each show has its own guidelines for submission. Some shows will not accept freelance work under any circumstances. (To find out which shows do accept freelance work, read *The Hollywood Reporter*. It routinely publishes this information in addition to the names, addresses and contact numbers of all the major television shows.) Don't waste your time sending a script to a show that doesn't want outside work; it will come back to you unopened. Some shows, especially those with longer runs, have what is called a *bible*. The bible of a show outlines all the pertinent character and plot information a writer needs to know in order to write a script. A bible is indispensable if you want to be successful. Usually, if a show accepts freelance work, you can ask for and receive a copy of one.

Shows like the *Star Trek* series have complex, detailed bibles. The legal department at Paramount Studios, where *Deep Space Nine* is produced, has an iron-clad rule that prevents anyone from the studio from reading an unsolicited story and script material. *Deep Space Nine* has a special arrangement, however, that allows them to consider freelance material: if it is submitted by a recognized agent registered with the Writers Guild of America, or, if it is submitted with an unaltered Paramount Television Release Form and submitted to:

> The Script Coordinator
> Star Trek: Deep Space Nine
> Paramount Pictures Corporation
> 5555 Melrose Ave., Hart 105
> Los Angeles, CA 90038-3197

(If you are considering submitting a *Deep Space Nine* script, you can get information about how to get a Paramount release form and a copy of the submission guidelines by calling (213) 956-8301.) No matter what studio you submit to, you shouldn't send scripts to the actors, producers, directors or anyone else associated with a program. All scripts have to come through the script coordinator.

The guidelines vary from show to show. For example, the *Deep Space Nine* guidelines will tell you that the staff won't read ideas, stories, outlines or treatments. They will only read completed scripts. They will also return *unread* any two-part scripts, so make sure your story fits into one hour.

Realistically Speaking

What are your chances of breaking through as a freelancer for television? If you don't have an agent, slim to none. To give you an idea of what you're up against if you decide to fly solo, the Writers Guild Television Market for June 1995 lists 104 shows in production for the 1995-1996 season. Of those 104 shows, only one—*Deep Space Nine*—is open for submissions from freelance writers without agents. *One*. Talk about fierce competition.

What happens to your odds if you do have an agent? Fifteen shows out of the 104 would accept submissions through agents. The odds aren't great, but they definitely improve. The other eighty-nine shows? Closed to submissions. Or as they put it, "All scripts committed for the current season."

These numbers are not finite: They rise and fall during the season, although not precipitously. The show list isn't all inclusive either. But you get the idea: television is a tough nut to crack from the outside.

A NOTE ABOUT THE SOAPS

You can say what you want about soap operas: that they're crass, base, exploitative, and have utterly no redeeming social value. You would never admit to watching them either. Well, somebody's watching them, lots of people, in fact.

How else would you explain the fact that a show like *The Guiding Light* has been on air for *forty* years? (Fifty-five years, if you count radio.) Other shows have similarly long runs. For years, the profits from soaps literally supported prime-time TV, but that's not so much the case anymore. In spite of dropping profits, however, the genre is still secure.

Those of you who are fans of the soaps may entertain a fantasy of becoming a writer for "daytime," as the group of shows is affectionately called. Before you rush off to New York City or Los Angeles to start knocking on doors, let me give you a snapshot of how these shows are written.

Stories for daytime are character driven. They thrive on their emotional content. Plots are devised to fit the characters rather than the opposite situation, in which the characters are slaves to the plot. According to writer James Houghton of *The Young and the Restless*: "Even while there's a mystery going on, it should have that emotional component. On a detective show, if there's a house burning down the guy's thinking, 'Who started it?' And in an adventure show, they're going to say, 'How are we gonna put this [fire] out?' But on a soap we're going to have a character say, 'God that makes me so sad to see that. All their mementos are gone.' "

You might have a mental image of a writer sitting in a room hashing out the story for the week, but the process of writing for daytime is very different from any other. Each show has its own way of doing things, but they share a basic approach.

A story begins with a head writer who creates the story line for thirteen or twenty-six weeks. The story line is segmented into daily episodes that outline the basic action for each day. Usually three plots—called the A, B and C plots—are running concurrently. The A plot is winding down, the B plot is in mid-stream, and the C plot is gearing up. Each story line is called a *breakdown*; each major action in the breakdown is called a *beat*.

The head writer then gives the beat sheet for the week to the outline writers, who organize each show. Once they have the go-ahead from the producer, the outline writers turn the material over to the dialogue writers.

John Boni, a writer for *General Hospital* gives us an insight into this complicated process: "There's an enormous mechanical component in putting a show together each week. It's truly a logistical puzzle. We have to consider which actors are on vacation, when sweeps are coming, how far to advance the story, how much to hold back, and what actor is complaining and wants a couple of extra scenes. The process involves an enormous amount of puzzle fitting, and trying to be creative within those constraints."

If a writer ever wanted to work with actors, this is one of the few places where it happens on a daily basis.

JOBS FOR WRITERS IN TELEVISION

Writers for episodic television have a much greater range of employment possibilities than a writer for features. The feature writer creates a script and is finished unless they are in the unique position of being a director or producer in addition to writing. But in television, a writer can hold any number of positions in the hierarchy of writers. In order from most important to least, they are:

The *executive producer* is usually the person who originated the concept for the series and oftentimes oversees the show in general. Richard and Esther Shapiro, for example, were the executive producers of *Dallas* and Linda Bloodworth-Thomason was the executive producer of *Designing Women* and *Love and War*.

The *supervising producer*, sometimes called a line producer, has more day-to-day responsibilities of making the show. While this person may be a writer, they also have to be production oriented.

The *producer* or *associate producer* is a person with a great title, but not usually a lot of responsibility. It's sometimes given as an honorarium.

The *executive story consultant* is a senior writer who's been in the trenches a year or two. Besides writing episodes, the executive story consultant also works with freelance writers and other staff writers.

Story consultants are sometimes part-timers who come in to rewrite scripts. The story consultant is not much different from an executive story consultant, except this person gets paid less money. Ditto the *story editor*, who makes even less money. The *term writer* writes episodes for the show; this is a starting staff position. Next, the *apprentice writer*, who is fresh off the boat and probably in the process of earning enough credits as a writer to join the Guild, makes even less than the other writers. Finally, there is the *freelance writer*, an outsider who writes for the show. A freelancer may have only one script or be contracted for multiple assignments.

Years ago I was offered a staff writing job by a Senior Vice President at Warner Brothers. He was also a very close friend. Knowing me, he offered the job but at the same time counseled me not to take it. He explained that the "shelf life" of staff writers is about three years, after which they burn out. It is intense, demanding work. It is financially rewarding, but you'd better be sure you're up to the rigors of writing on schedule, and a short schedule at that.

People often ask me why the quality of television is so bad. I don't claim to have the answer, because I don't think there is any one answer, but I do believe that the nature of television production itself is partially to blame. Let me explain.

You have an idea for a series. You sit down at the keyboard and write a pilot (the first program of a dramatic or comedy series, produced and presented to potential sponsors for series funding). Then you rewrite it, honing it until it has the perfect edge. The network loves the script and commits to the pilot. They also ask for outlines for twelve additional shows (or perhaps they only want a *short order* of six shows). You go back to the keyboard and develop story lines for the other shows.

Meanwhile the network makes and airs the pilot. The numbers (Nielson ratings) come back looking good. The network gives the series a go-ahead. It's now late in the year, and production for the series has to continue at full blast. The network is still being cautious, so it commissions three or maybe six episodes. They want to see how the series does before they'll approve more production. So you write the next episodes under the gun. You've already outlined the stories, so you have a head start. Now you wait.

Production is finished; the episodes have started to air. The Nielsons are holding up. The show isn't a hit, but it isn't a dog either. Week by week they study the figures as they come in. Finally, the studio green-lights either the rest of a half season or, if you wrote thirteen episodes, the *back nine* (which combine with the first thirteen to make a season of twenty-two shows). And what have you been doing in the meantime? Sitting on pins and needles, waiting for the studio to either kill the series or go with it. Suddenly it's a go, and you no longer have story outlines to rely on. The studio wants the additional episodes *now*, and the pressure is on. Even though the Guild allows three weeks for a writer to produce an hour of episodic television, that time frame won't work if you have to produce nine episodes. So you do what writers have always done when they don't have the time to be creative: rely on formulas. Stock characters and stock plots. That's one reason why a lot of television has a flatness about it.

One way out of that dilemma is to hire multiple writers or an *ensemble*. *M*A*S*H* was the first television show to successfully employ this innovative team approach; writers suddenly had time to think and be creative. This approach is now standard for many shows.

NOT ENOUGH TIME AND NOT ENOUGH MONEY

Another reason for the lack of quality of television is budget limitations. Most shows are *deficit financed*. That means that the network that approves the pilot for broadcast doesn't put up all the money to cover production costs. It puts up a majority, but the production company responsible for the show must now come up with the difference. Every show that premieres on television is a financial gamble, and the stakes are high. Producers with a track record of television success have an easier time raising the additional capital, but even for them it's an uphill struggle.

The payoff for the investors is the hope of syndication. After a show runs for a few seasons and accumulates a body of work (usually about a hundred episodes), then the production company can sell the syndication rights to independent stations. You've seen the second-run shows: reruns of *Cosby*, *M*A*S*H*, *Knight Rider* and *MacGyver*. With the expansion of the cable market, the demand for syndication is very high. Everything from *The Nostalgia Channel* to *Nick at Night* on Nickelodeon. Shows that have been collecting dust for years suddenly have new lives. Syndication rights can mean big money for the production company.

For shows just getting off the ground, however, that is a dream five or ten years down the road. In the meantime, money is tight, and that is reflected in the budget in the form of small casts, limited sets and effects, and simple plots. If you write for television, you're always working within a set of restrictions. Good writers know how to adapt and make the restrictions work for the show rather than against it. Lesser writers just throw up their hands and wonder why they ever wanted to write for television in the first place.

Another set of limitations for a show is called the show's *franchise*. The franchise is the gestalt of the program: who and what the characters are, what they do (and by extension what they don't do), and where they are. When I tune into my favorite show every week, I expect to see certain characters in certain situations in certain places. I know who these people are and I don't expect them to step out of character. That's not to say that change isn't possible for a show, of course it is, but it comes slowly over a period of weeks or even months. A writer must work within the confines of the franchise. You can't arbitrarily change the locale of Fraiser from Seattle, Washington to Topeka, Kansas. You also couldn't write an episode in which Frasier Crane is a rocket scientist or has a long-lost sister living in Bangor, Maine. The franchise states that Frasier Crane is a psychologist who works for a radio station in Seattle. He has a father, a brother named Niles, and a dog named Eddie. Those are the parameters for your story, and that is the franchise for the program. And there are other restrictions.

SUITABLE CONTENT. Network television is watchdogged by more groups than any other venue. That means there are subjects that are considered unsuitable for television. A lot has changed since the days of early television when you couldn't show a double bed or say the word *poignant* because it sounded too much like *pregnant*. Subjects that were formerly taboo now play regularly: domestic abuse, sexual abuse, adultery, homosexuality, and so on. But while writers are always pushing the edge of the envelope outward, the envelope is still definitely there. As often as the lines are redrawn, there are still lines that the writer cannot cross. The definition for what is tasteful remains forever slippery, but certain shows blazed the trail for others to follow: shows such as *All in the Family* and *Maude* for instance, which boldly addressed questions of homosexuality, abortion and racism.

STRUCTURE. Format and story structure are exact when it comes to episodic television. A half-hour program runs precisely twenty-two minutes of story. You can't be shorter or longer. An hour-long program is forty-five minutes. Breaks have to be in precise locations in order for the sponsors to advertise. Because it is so easy to channel surf with the remote, you have to end each segment with a *swing*, which is a dramatic moment that encourages the viewer to stay with the program over the commercial break. Many shows also have *teases* or *tags*, at the beginning and end of the show. Study the form that you're interested in; know it inside and out.

Television writers have to conform to two structures in the same script: the regular three-act dramatic structure and a structure which takes into consideration the shape of television time.

LANGUAGE. Keep it clean, period. An occasional "hell" or "damn" is acceptable for certain shows, but not any of what George

Carlin referred to as the "heavy seven"—the seven words in the English language that are forbidden on television.

PRIME-TIME PRIME

When cable first started to make headway into homes across America, theaters and networks alike feared that their numbers of viewers would plummet. The fear proved unfounded. Theater attendance actually went up, and while networks did lose some of their viewers, the numbers didn't drop as drastically as the naysayers predicted. Prime time television is still king.

The Writers Guild divides all of episodic television into four basic types of shows.

Episodic Drama

Sixty-minute format, shot on film. Roughly half of all shows in production (around fifty) are episodic dramas. Typical types are lawyer shows (*Matlock, Wright Verdicts*), police shows (*NYPD Blue, Homocide: Life on the Street, Law and Order*) and doctor shows (*ER, Chicago Hope*). These shows combine roughly four parts drama with one part comedy (the mix varies from show to show). The drama is often very intense, giving rise to the term *drama ovens* because of the overwhelming nature of the crises these people endure every hour.

Episodic dramas usually have three stories running through the hour. The main plot is the A story; the major subplot is the B story; and a minor subplot, often called a *runner*, is the C story. The runner may be a running gag or notion that recurs three times during the course of the hour: once in the first act, once in the second act, and once in the third act.

Episodic Comedy

Thirty-minute format, often shot on tape in studios before a live audience, but some are shot on film. Also known as the situation comedy or *sitcom*. Roughly half of all shows in production fall into this category as well. Usually sitcoms start the evening line-up followed later in the evening by the more serious episodic dramas.

Because it's nearly impossible to develop much of a plot in a half hour (that is, twenty-two minutes), the plots tend to be broad and simple. The show may have a major plot line (the A story) and a minor plot line (the B story), but may not have a runner. Each act tends to be between three and five complete scenes. Unlike situation dramas which have more expansive sets, situation comedies, especially those shot in studios, are limited to basic locations (the apartment, the place of business, etc.). Therefore the focus is not on action, but on the wittiness of the repartee between characters.

Someone once remarked that "Dying is easy. Comedy is hard." I don't know if comic writers are born or made (I suspect both), but you have to have the knack for comedy to be good at it. And that means timing. A good joke told badly will fall flat. Conversely, a bad joke told well can be funny. If you have a talent for writing comedy, this may be your niche. Good comic writers are in great demand.

You can always tell the writers on a set; they're the ones laughing so hard at their own jokes. Sometimes they're the only ones laughing. Great comedy seems spontaneous but is generally rehearsed. The stories of Charlie Chaplin's quest for perfection are legendary: He would do ten, twenty, as many as a hundred takes of a scene before he was satisfied. Try doing some shtick a hundred times and see if you still think it's funny. The Marx Brothers were also very well rehearsed. They would repeat a skit dozens upon dozens of times in order to refine and hone it. The true genius of comedy is to make the rehearsed seem spontaneous.

One page of television script translates to about forty-five seconds of screen time. During that time, you will be expected to produce anywhere from three to five solid jokes. Multiply that by the total number of pages in the half-hour and suddenly you have to come up with around two hundred jokes per show. Talk about torture. And these aren't just jokes you hear on the street; they are jokes that derive from the situation the characters find themselves placed in. They are jokes that build on each other, and that return over and over. A good writer knows how to exploit the comic nature of a situation. A good writer makes the ordinary seem strange, and the strange seem ordinary. Comedy is chaos; it subverts the social order. The Marx Brothers and the Three Stooges were anarchists: They took our most revered institutions and turned them into farces. In that sense, comedy is social satire.

Anthologies

Sixty- or thirty-minute format, shot on film or tape. The anthology series has always been popular on television. Whether it's highbrow, such as the *Hallmark Hall of Fame* or middlebrow such as the *Twilight Zone* and *Alfred Hitchcock Presents* or even lowbrow such as *Tales from the Darkside* and the *Tales from the Crypt*, audiences have always loved anthology series.

They come in every conceivable shade: from *Police Story* to *Amazing Stories* to *Love, American Style*.

The main distinguishing feature of the anthology series is that there is no continuing thread of plots or characters from week to week. Each show is an original teleplay. That's not to say that anthologies don't have franchises, because they do. The independently syndicated and enormously popular show *Tales from the Darkside* had a very specific franchise. Above the readily apparent theme of the show, which had to do with the macabre, the show relied on very specific common denominators. These denominators were critical to the show's success. While the writing of the shows wasn't about to garner an Emmy, it contained an abject lesson for all aspiring writers. The formula was simple:

1. Use a minimum cast. Preferably two cast members (protagonist and antagonist, but not always) and no more than four. Use either "no name" actors or "big name" actors who are willing to work for scale;

2. Use simple, preferably generic sets. Preferably no more than three. Nothing elaborate. Always use interiors in order to control conditions;

3. Rely more on dialogue than on action. Conflict tends to be verbal more often than physical;

4. Use special effects for climactic events, usually as part of the surprise twist at the end of the show.

This formula works well in a half hour format because you don't have enough time to develop much of anything except a (no pun intended) skeleton of a tale. The formula is a lot tougher to carry for a full hour because its demands on plot and character development are more rigorous. Other, larger budgeted shows, such as *Tales from the Crypt*, are traditionally shot on film rather than taped, can afford larger casts, more complex sets, exterior scenes, grander special effects and more physical action.

Anthology shows are a prime springboard for beginning actors and directors. Well-known actors who want to direct may start with a segment of an anthology show. (Rebecca DeMornay, for example, broke into directing on *Tales from the Crypt*.) If you look back at the credits of the original *Twilight Zone*, it reads like a Who's Who of Hollywood.

For freelancers, the anthology offers the greatest hope of selling a script.

Serials

Some serials are the soap operas of the evening. More elaborate than daytime television, the melodrama has a long tradition on television:

Dallas, Dynasty, Knott's Landing, Falcon Crest, and *The Monroes,* for example. Stories continue from week to week. The cliffhanger principle can still be surefire: the episode of *Dallas* that revealed who shot J.R. generated one of the largest television viewing audiences ever. We love melodrama; we love conniving villains—Joan Collins and Larry Hagman raised these roles to an art form—we also love good old-fashioned heroes and heroines who struggle with them. Melodramas are modern day vaudeville.

Other serials are less melodramatic. Steven Bochco broke ground with *Hill Street Blues* and *L.A. Law.* These types of shows are now a staple of prime time television. *NYPD Blue, ER* and *Murder One* are good examples.

Unlike episodic drama or comedy which tells a new story using the same characters and franchise from week to week, serials not only use the same characters but also continue plots from week to week. The dramatic structure may be similar to that of daytime soaps, using an A story, B story and C story within an hour. (Some shows may have as many as five or seven stories beginning, evolving, or ending in a given hour!)

Unlike traditional episodic television, in which a writer is free to exercise his or her imagination within the relatively flexible confines of the franchise, the dictates of a serial are much less flexible. They demand an intimate knowledge of the show's characters and the producer's intended direction for them during the season (the show's bible). As a result, serials tend to rely very heavily on their own staff writers rather than on freelancers.

PIE IN THE SKY

The question inevitably arises: What kind of money can I make writing for television? What you make depends upon your experience, of course, but if you're just breaking in or want to break in, there are some basic minimums (provided by the Writers Guild). You may not be a member of the Guild at first as an apprentice writer, but you'll quickly become one once you accumulate the requisite number of writing credits to join. (For complete information on this process, see the chapter on the Writers Guild.)

Writers who become attached to a show advance rapidly. Freelancers, when used, find themselves associated with certain story editors, producers and network executives. This process is normal in a business in which your next job always depends upon the quality of your contacts. It's easy to forget that as a freelance writer or even as a staff writer you don't have the same kind of job security most people have.

Most television shows don't last more than two or three seasons. A few go five, seven or ten years before they end. I once wrote for a show that had the distinction of being the shortest lived series on television: Two episodes and it was canceled. (Since that time, the record has been broken.) As a television writer you're at the mercy of the mysterious Nielsons, and what may be a spectacular success one week may become an abysmal failure the next. Television audiences are as notoriously fickle as they can be loyal. Therefore writers have to hedge their bets. If you see the numbers going south from week to week, it's time to start thinking about your future. What other show needs writers? Who do you know that's connected with other shows? Networking, we call it. Fanning the Rolodex. Never burn any bridges—chances are you could be headed back in that direction sooner or later.

The close-knitted nature of television has led people to believe that networks have their list of acceptable writers, sometimes called "the A list." Networks deny they have an exclusive list of writers. They do know certain writers by virtue of having worked with them in the past, and so they are inclined to prefer those writers over people whose work they don't know.

Nevertheless new writers are breaking into the inner circle all the time. Agents get through; other writers recommend new talent; and unsolicited scripts get through. It does happen; fresh blood is just as important to a network as old blood, if you'll forgive the metaphor.

For the sake of argument, let's say you've written a spec script that has caught the eye of a story editor. You make the sale. According to the Writers Guild *minimums*, you should get paid $12,000 for a half-hour script and $24,000 for a full hour for a prime-time network show. (This also assumes the story is original.)

Not bad you say; all I have to do is write four one-hour episodes a year, and I'll be raking in almost a hundred grand annually.

Wishful thinking for a newcomer. Landing four episodes on a show is possible, but not probable. And even if it does happen, you don't really make $96,000. This list of deductions is scary:

Agent's Commission of 10 percent	$ 9,600
Federal and State Taxes	
(35 percent bracket)	$28,800
Writers Guild Pension/Welfare Fund	$ 4,800

Your fat paycheck has just dwindled to $56,800.

This accounting is hypothetical. Rates go up with experience, and if you're on staff then you'll also be pulling down a weekly salary in addition to any scripts you may write. And then there are the rewrites, if you get them. Television is rewrite crazy. It's not unusual for a script to be rewritten five or even ten times, and not always by the same person. There's a saying in both television and theatrical features: "This is Tuesday; it needs a rewrite," a cynical way of saying that a script will get rewritten whether or not it needs to be rewritten.

So, you think, maybe I'd be better off writing a Movie of the Week.

MOWs

The Movie of the Week (MOW) is the brass ring on the carousel of network television. For some, there's no greater accomplishment than to write a MOW (and then win an Emmy for it). The Movie of the Week has been the backbone of network television since 1964 when the first one appeared on NBC. The MOW has its own slot, virtually always in the "movie bloc" of prime time (9-11 PM Eastern and Pacific time, 8-10 PM Central time). Because commercial television is so sponsor-driven, it pays the utmost attention to who is watching what at any given moment of the day. Demographers draw composites of the audience with the same painstaking care as insurance company actuaries. These viewer profiles are the rudder that guides the network ship: Everyone wants to know the age, sex, annual income and number of children of the viewers—a mass of detail that would put Big Brother's information requirements to shame.

If you've ever watched a MOW, then you already know its character is distinctly different from feature or cable films. As a writer you should be tuned in to the needs of the networks. The schizophrenia of Monday night is a good example. The male audience is typically watching Monday Night Football. Women who are free to choose their own program traditionally watch a MOW; the genre is specifically oriented towards a female audience.

Here are some ideas our theoretical writer wants to pitch to the network execs:

1. The true story about a downed American pilot who was stranded on an Pacific island swarming with Japanese soldiers during WWII for almost two years;

2. The true story of Custer's Last Stand at the Little Big Horn told

from the point of view of a Crow scout working for the Seventh Cavalry;

3. The true story of how Albert Einstein discovered the secret of the atomic bomb in 1942 and then hid the results from the U.S. Government;

4. The true story of Margaret Kinsett, a woman in Seattle, Washington, who lost custody of her three children when she was falsely accused by her estranged husband of abusing them.

You're looking at a slot for Monday night. Which of the four would you choose?

The first two stories would perhaps appeal more to males than to females. (Stories about WWII and cowboys and Indians don't exactly attract much of a female audience.) The story about Einstein may appeal to both sexes (although, as pitched, it is more male oriented). The story about the falsely accused mother, however, is clearly aimed at a female audience, but probably wouldn't interest many men.

If on Monday night, men are watching football, most women will want to watch something else. So you pick the movie that seems most clearly targeted towards women.

What if it's Tuesday night? Men are back in the mix. The film about Einstein, maybe. Maybe. Albert Einstein doesn't have much sex appeal. He may be too "intellectual." (I wouldn't dare guess at what point something becomes "too intellectual," but any discussion of atomic theory is certain to be the death knell of that idea.) Which then? The soldier, the Indian, the scientist or the accused mother?

Probably none of the above. We need another story, one which will appeal strongly to both sexes. The true story of a family in Junction City, Kansas, who blow the whistle on the owners of the pesticide plant that they've been working in for fifteen years. She gets cancer, and he gets fired. You have a wrenching tale of two people fighting not only for their own lives but for the lives of all their friends and neighbors as well.

Notice all five of the stories I've outlined were "true" stories. Stories based on facts. Stories taken out of today's headlines. Television likes to be immediate and it takes its lead from what's going on in the world around it. While my stories are not real, the stories that regularly appear in MOWs are taken in some part (large or small) from stories that make headlines. I don't know what "based on a true story" means. Is it 100 percent, 80 percent, 50 percent, or only 15 percent true? Unlike FDA guidelines that determine how much fruit juice must be in a drink before it can be called a fruit juice, there are no similar guidelines about how much fact must be in a story before it can be labelled "based on a true story." In some cases, it means a lot of the material is based on what really happened, and in other cases, well, the writer reshapes both characters and plot to make the material more "palatable."

Fiction is fiction. No claim has been made that the film is a documentary. "Based on a true story" is a lure to lend the film immediacy and legitimacy, but make no mistake about it—you're writing fiction. Because all writers take their notions of people, places and things from their own life experiences, you could make the claim that any story you write is in fact "based on a true story."

Television likes the charade, so don't overlook its strength. If a young man and his very pregnant wife get stranded in the desert, and he leaves her in a cave while he spends the next few days wandering around before he's found (and she's rescued), the story will have a very high public profile since it's already been covered by the mass media: newspapers, tabloids and talk shows. The recognition factor builds audience. Our curiosity for the off beat and the macabre is never fully satisfied.

But you can't unilaterally decide that you want to write the story of someone who's undergone an ordeal. You need to have their permission which may entail an option or outright sale of rights. Enter the agents and lawyers. These things have to be negotiated. Sometimes we know someone whose story would make an inspirational tale, and so we get permission to write the story. A bit of advice however: Don't test the strength of that relationship by not having everything in writing. Too many friendships and tempers have been lost because of assumptions. Everything needs to be spelled out *before* the stakes get big.

If you have the exclusive rights to a story or a bestseller that the networks want (because of a unique or high profile), then you can be in a position to negotiate a project. A typical network two-hour MOW pays a minimum of $32,000 for both the script and story, but networks have been known to engage in a feeding frenzy for some projects. Prices can and do skyrocket. Let the professionals (i.e., your agent) negotiate for you.

Another angle: Frequently television actors have contracts with networks that guarantee them a set number of shows over a certain time span. Let's say a well-known actress has negotiated a deal to act in three television movies over the next four years. Her contract will likely have a "play or pay" provision that ensures that she will be paid whether or not a project gets underway. (Ever hear of a writer who got paid for *not* writing a script?) While the financial end of it may be satisfying, professionally it's more important for an actor to be on the screen. Actors would rather work. Therefore actors and actresses are actively seeking roles. A savvy writer might work with a particular actor or actress in mind.

Which brings up the WIJ (Woman In Jeopardy) film, a favorite theme of MOWs. The formula is simple, yet powerful. A woman is overwhelmed by a menacing figure, who's generally and somewhat comically portrayed as a psychopathic, two-timing, lying, thieving man. The woman is victim; the man is victimizer. (This formula speaks directly to the core fantasy of power for women.) The woman will find the strength to fight back, and justice, in one form or another, will be served. Our example of the woman who loses custody of her children to her estranged husband is a case of WIJ.

Whatever approach you take, your competition for a MOW will be fierce. Each network hears about a hundred pitches a week for MOWs. Top producers, directors and actors routinely get shot down. Of every hundred projects that a network might buy for development, less than twenty will make it to the screen. The MOW market is a very tough nut to crack.

But persistence is a virtue.

The Mini-Series

Some series have made television history. *Roots* and *Shogun* were landmarks for their quality and their technical prowess. Most mini-series, however, are forgettable. Mini-series usually start out as a book with a proven track record, like those by Sidney Sheldon, Jackie Collins and Stephen King. The mini-series, which traditionally runs about four hours over two or three nights, is the realm of the experienced writer. Newcomers need not apply *unless* by some stroke of luck or cunning you have the rights to the original work. Better spend your time writing spec scripts.

BREAKING IN

Breaking in means getting your foot in the door. Letters rarely do it. Writing a spec script might do it, but the odds are against you. If you really want in, then you'll have to do some homework.

First, *know the show*. Know the franchise, know who the writers are and what they've written, and be conversant with the season (and previous seasons). Make it clear you've dedicated your life to studying this show; it's not a hobby, it's a passion.

Second, *make contact*. Call a story editor or a writer. If possible, have lunch with them. You want to learn more; you want them to know you intend to end up working on the show, whatever it takes.

Third, *have a spec script*. Make sure you understand both format and dramatic structure. Each show has its own particular quirks, so make sure you include them in your script. Imitate the style you admire most. Show anyone who is willing to look that, "Hey, I can do this too! I belong here!"

Fourth, *commit*. If you're trolling (looking for a job on any program that will hire you), it'll show. Make it clear that you don't want to work for any other show, the only job you want is for this particular one. And be convincing.

There are a lot more opportunities for writers in television than in the theatrical market. But you have to make a decision about which path you intend to pursue, because this fork in the road (television or theatrical) is a hard one to reverse. Television writers rarely write feature scripts and vice versa. Call it typecasting. The barrier is invisible but very real, and it holds true for producers, directors and actors too. Breakthroughs, as they're called, are rare. So make your decision accordingly.

Chapter Fourteen

Inside the Script

The first twelve chapters of this book deal with the business of handling your script; this chapter deals exclusively with its form.

The first question is the only one of any significance: Is form as important as content in scriptwriting? (By form I am referring to script format: the elaborate set of rules that require things be written in a certain way.)

The question forces the issue by requiring a "yes" or "no" answer, but I'd say, "Yes, definitely, form is as important as content."

The problem with trying to equate form and content is that content is critical in its way just as form is critical in its, but the two aren't comparable. You can overlook a weak form if the content is brilliant, but you can't overlook lousy content however brilliant the form.

Don't let anyone tell you that script format isn't important, because it is. Beginning writers are easily daunted by the myriad of abbreviations, formulas, rules, laws and quirks that are found in virtually every script. There's a lot to learn (although these details are easier to deal with now that there are a dozen different software programs that create the format for you). The writer's hackles rise: Why should I learn all these silly rules?

Script format has been evolving for over half a century. Although the logic behind the rules may not be immediately apparent, there is almost always a purpose. Don't forget that a script doesn't just talk to a reader; it must also talk to the director, the production designer, the actors, the editor, the special effects people, the sound people, the lighting people and many others. You must learn several vocabularies so that your intentions are clear.

The problem with most of the format books that I've read is that they tell you what to do, but not *why* you should do it. If someone had taken the time to explain the reason why certain words are capitalized and others are not, then you wouldn't resent doing it. As it is, the rules seem capricious if not downright perverse. This chapter will take you through the five major pieces of a script and explain how to deal with them and more importantly, why you should play by the rules.

STORY AT A GLANCE

Writing a script is a juggling act. The main focus of the script has to be story. Anything that interferes with the telling of the story, hurts the story. Without question, the most serious mistake writers make when writing a script is to clutter the story with an endless stream of details about camera angles, directions to the director, directions to the actors, and directions to everybody on the set. The result of all this script "static" is that the story gets lost in all the production details.

If you're concerned with how your film is going to look and how the actor should deliver your lines and what kind of clothes the actors should be wearing, then you don't have your mind on the story. You should be a director or an art director or a dialogue coach. Remember the old adage, Shoemaker, stick to your last? The saying applies equally well here. Writer, stick to your story. Everything else is extraneous detail. *If you write something and it neither advances the plot nor develops character, then it doesn't belong.* Period. Even if you don't read another word in this chapter, you'll now know all you need. The strength of any good script is the quality of its story, not what kind of camera angles you think the DP should use.

SCENE AND SUMMARY

A fiction writer is used to two types of narrative: scene and summary. The difference between the two is as simple as it is dramatic.

In summary, the author recounts the action from a distance:

The doctor tells Lilly that her son, Roy, has an internal hemorrhage. Lilly looks so young, the doctor can't believe Roy is Lilly's son, but Lilly is more concerned about Roy. She asks the doctor if he knows who she works for. When he says he does, Lilly tells the doctor she'll have him killed if he doesn't make her son better. The doctor watches in shock as Lilly leaves in the ambulance with her son.

In scene, however, the writer puts the reader in the action as it happens:

EXT. MADERO APARTMENTS - DAY

Roy, unconscious, is wheeled on a gurney towards an ambulance, accompanied by Lilly and the DOCTOR, a nervous heavyset man in his fifties trying to maintain a false heartiness.

> DOCTOR
>
> I just can't believe this strapping young man can be your son.

> LILLY
>
> Never mind that. Just take care of him.

> DOCTOR
>
> Mrs. Dillon, your son has had an internal hermorrhage, he's bleeding to death inside.

> LILLY
>
> Well, make it stop!

> DOCTOR
>
> His blood pressure is under a hundred. I don't think he'll live to get to the hospital.

> LILLY
> (icy, stern)
> You know who I work for.

(*He's uncomfortable, wants to dismiss that part of his life.*)

> DOCTOR
>
> Yes, yes, but that's . . .

> LILLY
>
> My son will be all right. If he isn't, I'll have you killed.

Lilly follows Roy into the ambulance. The door closes. The ambulance drives off, leaving the doctor, in shock, staring after it.
(from *The Grifters*, screenplay by Donald E. Westlake, based on the novel by Jim Thompson)

A screenplay is in the here and now. The action is immediate, vivid and alive; the characters always speak for themselves rather than through the omniscient voice of the author. A scene is in the moment; it's happening now, even if it's a flashback or a dream.

A script is made of scenes. Each scene has four major types of information that relay the story: *scene headings*, *stage direction*, *dialogue* and *personal direction*.

Scene Headings

The *scene heading* contains very specific, basic information about a scene. It always comes at the beginning, or head, of each scene, and the information is *always* capitalized. In the scene from *The Grifters*, the scene heading is:

EXT. MADERO APARTMENTS - DAY

A scene heading follows a very specific order of information. That information is organized according to three basic components: (1) *where*; (2) *when*; and (3) *what/who*. A trained person "drinks in" scene headings. It makes sense, therefore, for you to keep the information very specific. Include only information that is critical to understanding the scene; anything else is too much.

WHERE. The first bit of information the reader sees is an abbreviation that indicates whether the scene is an interior (indoor) or an exterior (outdoor) shot. These locations are always indicated either by the abbreviation INT. or EXT. The scene from *The Grifters* is, therefore, outdoors (EXT.).

The second bit of information elaborates the "where" of the scene. We know from the scene that it is outdoors, but that is too vague. Therefore, the writer gives a short description of the location. In this case, the scene is taking place outdoors at the Madero Apartments. (Exactly what the Madero Apartments are is clear in the context of the story.)

You may also include additional information about the location as it relates to time. For example, you may need to clarify the year (if it isn't contemporary) or the season of the year, or the exact time of day. This information is always included in parentheses. For example:

EXT. NEW YORK CITY (SPRING)
INT. THE WHITE HOUSE (1865) - THE OVAL OFFICE
INT. PEARL HARBOR (6:10 AM)

Remember, these specific details are necessary to understanding the where (and part of the when) of the scene; you include specifics of time (such as year, season or time of day) only as it relates to location.

WHEN. "When" means "what time of day." In its simplest form, the day is divided into two segments: DAY and NIGHT. If it's not important what time of day the action happens, then you should just write DAY as in the example from *The Grifters*.

If the action takes place at night, then write NIGHT. Be careful about using night scenes, however, because they're much more expensive to shoot. Night scenes usually require extra pay for the crew, extra people, extra lighting, generators and other equipment. A night scene can cost two or three times what it would cost to do the same scene during the day. So make certain there's a good reason why that scene should be shot at night.

Let's add time to the scene headings from the previous section:

EXT. NEW YORK CITY (SPRING) - DAY
INT. THE WHITE HOUSE (1865) - THE OVAL OFFICE -
    NIGHT
INT. PEARL HARBOR (6:10 AM) - DAWN

WHAT/WHO. This category gives us an idea of what the subject of the camera is. It may be a person or thing:

EXT. NEW YORK CITY (SPRING) - DAY - EMPIRE STATE
    BLDG.
INT. THE WHITE HOUSE (1865) - THE OVAL OFFICE -
    NIGHT - PRESIDENT LINCOLN
INT. PEARL HARBOR (6:10 AM) - DAWN - U.S.S. ARIZONA

CAMERA ANGLE. I haven't included the camera angles in my description of what is included in scene headings. The reason for that, which should be obvious based upon what John McTiernan and Andy Laszlo have said earlier in this book, is that writers shouldn't concern themselves with the details of camera shots and movement. But it would be remiss of me not to tell you that camera angles are traditionally included in the scene headings.

There's no law that says that you can't include them, but if you do, remember, you are treading upon someone else's ground. The writer may suggest, but the director or the DP is not obliged to follow. Some even resent the writer's interference. Make certain that if you do include a camera angle, that you have an important reason for doing so. If it's an ordinary description of a shot, then there's no reason to include it. But if you have a really special way of seeing the scene; make your suggestion. And remember, a little goes a long way. If you're a frustrated director, now's *not* the time to try to show off.

If you're bound and determined to include camera angles in your scene headings then they're included between the time of day and the subject of the camera:

EXT. NEW YORK CITY (SPRING) - DAY - FULL SHOT -
   EMPIRE STATE BLDG.
INT. THE WHITE HOUSE (1865) - THE OVAL OFFICE -
   NIGHT - CLOSE-UP - PRESIDENT LINCOLN
INT. PEARL HARBOR (6:10 AM) - DAWN - LONG SHOT -
   U.S.S. ARIZONA

Once you've established a location and you have a series of scenes that take place in the same location, you don't have to keep repeating yourself. Use logic; if the reader knows where you are in the story, don't repeat needless information. There are short cuts that help you reduce the amount of information in a scene heading. For a complete treatment of them, I recommend *The Complete Guide to Standard Script Formats, Part I: The Screenplay* by Hillis Cole Jr. and Judith Haag (CMC Publishing). For television formats, get the companion volume, *Part II: Taped Formats for Television* by Judith Haag. These two books have everything you need to know to format a script.

Stage Direction

Stage direction usually comes immediately after the scene heading and at any time throughout a scene. As a writer, you get to tell your story only in two places: dialogue and stage direction, so any part of your story that isn't included in what your characters say is included in the stage direction.

Normally stage direction includes information about the movements of the characters and their mental states. Look at the scene from *The Grifters* again. The paragraph following the scene heading is stage direction:

> Roy, unconscious, is wheeled on a gurney toward an ambulance, accompanied by Lilly and the DOCTOR, a nervous heavy-set man in his fifties trying to maintain a false heartiness.

We learn what characters are present in the scene, where they are, and what they're doing. Roy and Lilly are continuing characters and have appeared in previous scenes, but the doctor is a new character. When a *major* character appears for the first time, you should capitalize the name or role if the character has no name (e.g., DOCTOR). By capitalizing the name (or role) you alert the actor that this is his first appearance. He doesn't have to page back any further to find out where he enters. This time saving device helps production staff and actors find their way around the script more easily.

You would also capitalize *sound cues*. Whenever you describe a sound *that isn't made by a human being* (such as sirens, bells, crashes) you should capitalize the sound. In the final stage direction, when the ambulance leaves, if you had decided to include the siren wailing, then it would read like this:

> Lilly follows Roy into the ambulance. The door is closed. The ambulance drives off, SIREN screaming, leaving the doctor, in shock, staring after it.

By capitalizing the sound cue, you alert the sound staff that it will have to provide the sound. Remember, this applies only to mechanical sounds, not sounds that can be made by the actors.

Stage direction can appear as often in a scene as you believe it's necessary. Notice that stage direction appears twice more in the scene: once when the writer wants to describe how the doctor feels when Lilly brings up the issue of her employer (which makes him uncomfortable), and again at the end of the scene, when Lilly leaves in the ambulance and leaves the doctor in shock.

If you have a particularly long stage direction, break it up into paragraphs to make it more readable. *Avoid large blocks of print in your screenplay*.

Donald Westlake does a good job addressing only issues of story in his stage direction. Too many writers clutter up their stage direction with descriptions of everything from special effects to technical descriptions for sound or camera. These needless details bog down the story. Forget the technical stuff; leave it to the professionals. Just tell the story.

Dialogue

The rules for dialogue are simple. Notice that the dialogue falls into an imaginary box in the middle of the page. In fact, if you fold the page in half lengthwise, the crease should fall on the first letter of the characters name (known as a *character cue*).

The rules for dialogue are designed to help the actor. For instance, you should never break a sentence from one page to the next. Always stop at the end of a sentence. This format provides the actor with a natural break.

If a character's speech should get broken between two or more pages, you need to let the actor know that there's more dialogue on the next page by including the word *MORE* at the bottom of the last line of dialogue. Let's say the scene we've been using falls on two pages. This is how you should break the page:

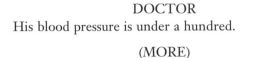

DOCTOR

His blood pressure is under a hundred.

(MORE)

- -

DOCTOR (CONT'D)

I don't think he'll live to get to the hospital.

The actor now knows that his speech is continued from the first page to the next page. You may say to yourself, well, that's obvious, isn't it? All he has to do is turn the page. Actors don't carry the entire script around; they carry pages with the scenes they're working on. If, by mistake, someone should forget the last page and the dialogue didn't include the word (MORE) at the end of the speech, the actor would think that was his last line. But the fact that (MORE) is there lets him know his speech isn't over yet.

The principle works in reverse too. You should repeat the character cue on the second page with the abbreviation *CONT'D* in parentheses to let the actor know that his speech started on a *previous* page. This way, an actor knows for sure his speech is complete.

Avoid long speeches. If you have a character that has to go on at length, break up the dialogue with stage direction or interjections from other characters. Since dialogue is such a dominant part of a screenplay, writers sometimes get lost in the "voices," which is sometimes called "voices in the void." That means you're guilty of having a lot of dialogue but very little sense of the physical world around the characters. What are they doing while they're talking? What are the important physical details that add a sense of place and mood? A screenplay shouldn't be dialogue heavy any more than it should be stage direction heavy. Find a balance between the two that allows you to tell the story and yet keep a strong sense of the physical and emotional world that your characters are in.

Some other rules:

- Spell out all one and two digit numbers (one, ten, twenty, fifty) but use numbers for 100 and over.

- Spell out all personal titles except for Mr., Mrs. and Ms.
- Spell out all indications of time: ten-thirty, not 10:30.
- Spell out "okay," not OK or o.k.
- When in doubt, spell it out.

The reason for these rules is to help the timing of a page. There is a loose rule in screenplays that one page of script equals one minute of screen time. While this doesn't hold for every page, it does tend to even out over the course of the script. Some wise person discovered that spelling out words helped maintain this pacing.

Personal Direction

Personal direction indicates to the actor how you think a certain line or speech should be read. In the scene from *The Grifters*, Westlake uses personal direction once in the scene.

> LILLY
> (icy, stern)
> You know who I work for.

Personal direction always appears in parentheses below the character cue (in this case, LILLY) The writer wants the actor to know that she should read the line with this kind of emotion.

Again, character cues should be used sparingly. Actors don't like writers telling them how to act anymore than directors or cinematographers like to be told how to do their jobs. The rule of thumb is simple: If the emotional context of the speech is obvious, then refrain from giving personal direction. If, however, you think the line should be played in a way that isn't immediately apparent, then by all means suggest it.

The wrong way:

> TRACY
> (angrily)
> Get the hell out of my way!

You don't have to be a genius to figure out that Tracy is angry with a line like that. Better to leave out the personal direction. However, perhaps you believe that Tracy's threat would sound more sinister if she were tired or disgusted, so you give a key word or two after the character cue to give the character insight the actor will need. Of course, telling the actor how she should read it is no guarantee that's how she'll do it, either.

The right way:

> TRACY
> (wearily)
> Get the hell out of my way!

Let's return for a moment to Lilly's line: "You know who I work for." Ask yourself if it was necessary for Westlake to include the personal direction (icy, stern). I don't think so. If Lilly's line had been a question rather than a declarative statement ("You know who I work for?") then I would agree with the inclusion of the personal direction. But because the line is declarative, it carries the threat with it, so the actor would naturally make the line sound threatening. That would make the personal direction redundant. Nit-picking, sure, but it illustrates my point.

As with stage direction and dialogue, less is more. Save it for when you really need it. If you overuse personal direction, the director and actors tend to tune it out altogether.

A good screenplay balances all these elements in healthy proportions to each other. Too much of any one thing is no good. Frustrated directors tend to overdo the stage direction, and frustrated actors tend to overdo the personal direction. The single most important thing to remember is that you shouldn't include anything that interferes with the telling of your story.

AUTO-FORMAT

Personal computer software programs are now available that will automatically make your script conform to industry standard formats. Called format programs or script processors, these programs provide multiple formats (film, TV, audio-visual and so forth) that automatically position script elements in their proper places.

Among many other features, they can break the pages where needed, add necessary MORE and CONT'D cues, and provide help. Some have advanced features such as the ability to provide a list of scenes and even shuffle the scenes for a different version of your story. More importantly these script processors align the slugline (Scene Heading), character cues, stage direction, action, transitions and other script elements properly. For the working writer, these functions can improve your efficiency while minimizing stress during revision.

Software is available in two styles. One style is an "add on" program that works in conjunction with your existing word processor. The other is a stand-alone program. Both have their good and bad points but ultimately the choice you make boils down to your personal preference. Both styles are available in Macintosh or IBM-compatible versions.

Sorting through the software advertisements can be confusing and time consuming. But make your choice carefully; you may regret a quick decision. Even getting advice from well-meaning friends isn't always the best way to make a decision; what works for them may not work for you. A professionally trained sales consultant may be able to help you identify a particular program that most closely matches your personal strengths, weaknesses and tastes. Fortunately, many of the software companies will give you a free demo program so that you can "try before you buy." I wouldn't buy any software without first trying it on your own computer at your own pace.

Some computer consultants and retail stores offer not only demonstrations of their hardware and software programs but also help with installation, training and tutoring, repairs, technical and even moral support. In Los Angeles, one store has lined its walls with framed movie posters that have been autographed by the screenwriters who thank the people there for their help getting them started with software.

For whatever software package you decide to buy, know what level of support you can get from your vendors. Technical assistance is not available from all software manufacturers, so check carefully.

Software programs are frequently reviewed in many of the trade publications such as *The Journal of the Writer's Guild of America, West*; *Screenwrite Now!* and *Hollywood Reporter*. *Essential Software for Writers* by Hy Bender (Writer's Digest Books, 1994) gives a complete description of most of the programs in addition to story development software, software available on CD-ROM and online services.

The following list of sources may not be complete, and new products are being released all the time, so stay alert.

The Writer's Computer Store
11317 Santa Monica Blvd.
Los Angeles, CA 90025
(800) 272-8927; (310) 479-7774
FAX (310) 477-5314

ScriptWizard
Stephani Warren & Associates
The Warren Script Applications
3204 Dos Palos Dr.
Los Angeles, CA 90068
FAX (310) 874-6028

Scriptware
Cinovation, Inc.
1750 Thirtieth St., Suite 360
Boulder, CO 80301-1005
(800) 788-7090; (303) 786-7899
FAX (303) 786-9292

Scriptor
Screenplay Systems
150 E. Olive Ave., Suite 203
Burbank, CA 91502-1849
(818) 843-6557; FAX (818) 843-8364

ScriptThing
ScriptPerfection Enterprises
3061 Massasoit Ave.
San Diego, CA 92117-7515
(800) 450-9450; (619) 270-7515

Movie Master
Comprehensive Cinema Software
148 Veteran's Dr.
Northdale, NJ 07647
(800) 526-0242; (201) 767-7990
FAX (201) 767-7377

SuperScriptPro
Inherit the Earth Technologies
1800 S. Robertson Blvd., Suite 326
Los Angeles, CA 90035
(310) 559-3814
FAX (310) 559-3814

▪ Chapter Fifteen ▪

Inside Plot

The industry finds life a lot simpler if it divides stories into two categories: A script is either plot driven or it is character driven.

THE PLOT-DRIVEN STORY

A plot-driven story is one in which the events take precedence over the characters, as a result the characters become secondary to the action. Albert ("Cubby") Brocolli pioneered the prototypical plot-driven movie with his series of James Bond films, which are still being made after thirty-five years, an excellent example of box-office stamina.

The easiest way to identify a plot-driven story is to look at the main character. Plot-driven characters are essentially static: They're the same at the end of the film as they were at the beginning. They don't change as people: They're frozen in time and space as a sort of mythic or archetypal hero. James Bond never changes (except faces, now and then); Indiana Jones never changes; and neither do the basic stock of characters played by Steven Seagal, Chuck Norris, Jean-Claude Van Damme or any of the stable of action heroes we flock to the theaters to see. Character development isn't important in the movies: what's important is the satisfaction of movement, which usually takes the shape of car chases, train wrecks, shootouts, stampedes, warriors in battle in the street or on the field, and fireworks on an ever-growing scale. What's important is that good triumphs over evil and that justice is served. We get a certain satisfaction out of seeing our value system justified dramatically over and over.

Plot-driven films are works of the body rather than of the mind. The audience gets restless when people talk too much or sit still for too long. The movie experience is visceral rather than intellectual. These films speak to our unconscious needs, whether it be the triumph of love or revenge. We don't want to think; we want to feel these movies.

A good action film is kinesthetic. Technically, kinesthesia is the sensation of position and movement in the viewer's body as it's perceived through the nerve ends in our muscles, tendons and joints. If you've ever seen the high speed car chase on the hills of San Francisco in *Bullitt* with Steve McQueen or the runaway ore car sequence in *Indiana Jones and the Temple of Doom*, then you know what I'm talking about. The point of view is so engaging that you'll find yourself leaning into the curves and bracing yourself when the car torpedoes over a hill or around a curve. (The effect is more pronounced on the big screen; television diminishes kinesthesia by reducing the scale.) Vicariously, you're sitting in the seat next to Steve McQueen or Harrison Ford, and you feel the speed, the vibration and the bone-crunching jolts.

The so-called action director specializes in this kind of plot, some examples are James Cameron in *The Terminator*, Ridley Scott in *Alien*, John McTiernan in *Die Hard* and *The Hunt for Red October* and Andrew Davis in *Under Siege*.

THE CHARACTER-DRIVEN STORY

The character-driven plot, on the other hand, concentrates attention on the people in the story rather than the action. Whereas plot-driven stories are physical, the character-driven plot is emotional. They're stories of the mind rather than the body. Events are secondary to the people. An action hero is the same at the end of the film, but the hero (or anti-hero) of a character-driven film has undergone internal change by the end of the film. Instead of character following action, here character development predominates. We're interested in the people first. We're interested in what the characters do because their actions reveal who they are. Interpreting action helps us understand the motives of people. In an action film, we don't have to do that kind of work. The characters are pre-shaped for us, and we know who they are and what they stand for before we even begin. In the character film, however, we focus our attention on the people and try to understand the who, what and why of them. We never have to ask why James Bond or Indiana Jones does anything; we know their characters and motives by heart. They are drawn with broad strokes that make distinguishing good and evil, ugly and beautiful very easy.

But the human condition is much more complex, and sometimes we want to explore this territory and try to learn what it means to be human. Black and white give way to perpetual gray. Certainty and righteousness give way to moral dilemma. Tolstoy pointed out that "good versus bad" is easy to write, but real stories aren't about good versus bad. Real stories are about "good versus good"—people who find themselves caught up in situations that have no clear right or wrong answer.

A true moral dilemma provides the structure for a character-driven plot. It provides inspiration and energy. (For more discussion on developing structure in your work and more clearly defining your plot, see *Twenty Master Plots and How to Build Them*, Writer's Digest Books.) The plot-driven story has a moral dilemma as well, but it's almost always bipolar, which means there are two choices: good or evil, right or wrong. But in a character-driven story, we're on more uncertain ground. The audience shares in the dilemma: What would you do in the same circumstance?

The example I'm about to give you isn't from a film; it's from a college course in situational ethics. The problem is profound and it's real. The problem takes on dimension not in the abstract, but in the concrete, when it has to apply to a person's choice of how to act. That's the substance of a character-driven story.

First, the scenario:

You're a transplant surgeon. You've just received word that a heart is available for transplant from a donor that died in an car accident. Four of your patients are qualified for the transplant. They are:

1. A twelve-year old girl, the only child of a middle-class family;
2. A thirty-seven year old father of three teenagers who's a boatyard worker that makes $12.75 an hour;
3. A forty-two-year-old homeless woman who's an alcoholic;
4. A fifty-year-old man who is the chief executive officer of a company that employs several hundred people (and, who, incidentally is willing to pay $250,000 for the transplant—money that could be used to help save other lives).

As the attending surgeon, you're responsible for choosing which of your patients gets the transplant. Which person do you choose and why?

The person you choose will reveal a lot about who you are and the way you think. Your choice will reflect your social biases. A valid, compelling and logical argument can be made for any of the four patients, and yet you have to decide that one of the patients deserves the transplant more than the others. Some people may argue that the little girl has the most life to live and therefore ought to get the transplant; others will argue that the boatyard worker should get the transplant because four others depend upon him and because he seems to be a productive, hard-working member of society; yet others would argue that the homeless alcoholic woman should get the heart because she is so underprivileged; and yet others would argue in favor of the CEO, citing the fact that hundreds of other people rely on him for their livelihoods, and, futhermore, a quarter of a million dollars can lead directly to saving other lives.

Just as you can argue for any of the candidates, so can you argue against any of them. If you chose the young girl, you might be guilty of discriminating on the basis of age; if you chose the boatyard worker, you might be guilty of discriminating on the basis of class; if you chose the homeless woman, you might be guilty of reverse discrimination by choosing someone of no apparent social worth; and if you chose the CEO you might be guilty of discriminating in favor of the rich. As you can see the issue reflects the hopes and fears of society.

So in your character-driven script, you create a doctor, give her a name and a hospital, and put her to the test. We meet each of the four patients; suddenly they have names, pasts and presents, and it's up to the doctor to decide what their futures will be. She hates being forced into the role of playing God, and yet she must act. Whatever decision she makes, however much she agonizes over it, she will be simultaneously right and wrong. She will have to pay a price for whatever decision she makes: There is no clear way through this dilemma.

In a character-driven story we focus on the doctor. We want to know who she is and why she makes the decision she makes. We want to know what the decision does to her. Does the burden of such responsibility demoralize and crush her? Or does she rise through the chaos to become a stronger, more confident woman? The story becomes a testing ground for ideas; abstractions get faces, and what had started out as a mind game now takes on a deeper, more profound quality. Our doctor will be a different person by the end of the story. She'll either grow or wither as the result of the experience. This is the true potential of a character-driven story.

A QUICK STUDY

With the coming of the technological age in films, the plot-driven film overtook the character-driven film. We're still fascinated with expensive toys; in the kingdom of moviemaking, the computer still reigns.

In the thirties and forties however, the opposite was true. Actors were under contract to studios and therefore available pretty much at the whim of the execs, who were concerned more with the creation of a standardized product than the creation of memorable cinema art. Perhaps only by default, the studio chiefs managed to accomplish both.

The films of this period have a lot to teach us about character. Here's a list of memorable character films listed by year. How many of them have you seen?

1930: *All Quiet on the Western Front*
1931: *Doctor Jekyll and Mr. Hyde*
1932: *Scarface*
1933: *The Invisible Man*
1934: *David Copperfield*
1935: *Les Miserables*
1936: *Rembrandt*
1937: *The Prisoner of Zenda; Lost Horizon*
1938: *Alexander Nevsky; Pygmalion*
1939: *Gone With the Wind; Stagecoach; The Hunchback of Notre Dame; Mr. Smith Goes to Washington*
1940: *The Grapes of Wrath; Rebecca*
1941: *Citizen Kane; The Maltese Falcon*
1942: *Casablanca; The Magnificent Ambersons*
1944: *Henry V; Double Indemnity*
1945: *Brief Encounter; The Lost Weekend*
1946: *Great Expectations; Gilda; The Best Years of Our Lives*
1947: *Crossfire*
1948: *Oliver Twist; The Naked City*
1949: *The Third Man*

I don't mean to infer that the good character films were only made during this time frame. Many other good character films have been made since: *On the Waterfront* (1954), *Marty* (1955), *Twelve Angry Men* (1957), *The Hustler* (1961), *Lawrence of Arabia* (1962), *Hud* (1963), *Andrei Rublev* (1966), *Bonnie and Clyde* (1967), *Butch Cassidy and the Sundance Kid* and *Midnight Cowboy* (1969), *The Godfather* (1972), *Chinatown* (1974), *One Flew Over the Cuckoo's Nest* (1975), *Annie Hall* (1977), *The Chant of Jimmy Blacksmith* (1978), *Raging Bull* (1980) and many others. No doubt you feel I've left out other important films; making a complete list is impossible. But character-based films have always been a staple of our cinematic diet, and profit capacity notwithstanding, they will continue to be.

MORE CHOICES

Should you write a plot- or a character-driven story? There are good reasons for choosing either.

Reasons for writing a plot-driven story:

- The industry loves genre pictures; as a whole, they're much more commercially viable than character-driven stories. (Translation: they make big bucks at the box office and therefore are easier to sell.)
- They tend to be formulaic in terms of structure and characters and therefore easier to write.
- They're bigger budget pictures and appeal to a wider audience than character-driven pictures.
- It's easier to "slot" or cast actors and directors for plot-driven stories.
- They pay a *lot* better than character-driven pictures.

Reasons for *not* writing a plot-driven story:

- They tend to be formulaic in terms of both structure and characters. (It's tough to be original when the same film has already been written a thousand times.)
- The competition is fierce, and right now Hollywood favors big-name writers over no-name writers.
- Budgets for action pictures run from high to very high which further reduces the chances of selling your script.
- Plot-driven stories are less forgiving when it comes to weaknesses in plot. They must be crafted extraordinarily well.

Reasons for writing a character-driven story:

- More freedom to explore complex issues and the nature of what it means to be human in our world.
- More freedom to explore your own personal agendas.
- Lower budgets mean lower financial risks which increases the possibilities for selling your script, especially if you write a story in the low-budget range (between $5 and $8 million).
- Certain actors and directors hunger for this kind of material. It showcases their talent, and some of them will work for minimums just to do a solid piece of work. It may act as a launching pad for a starting actor or director; it may give the B-list actor the extra push needed to increase their "stock" as a dramatic performer; or it may give an A-list actor a chance to break out of typecasting. For instance, Bruce Willis

has been typecast as an action hero because of the *Die Hard* films and *Hudson Hawk*, but he showed some dramatic range in his minor role as a boxer in *Pulp Fiction*.

■ Character-driven stories are more forgiving when it comes to plot deficiencies. Because our attention is focused on the characters, details of plot don't seem as important as they are in a plot-driven story.

■ A good character-driven story is always a good portfolio piece to show off your talent as a writer even if it doesn't sell.

Reasons for *not* writing a character-driven story:

■ Although Hollywood clamors for well-written character pieces, as a general rule they don't do nearly as well at the box office as action films. Well-written and well-acted films such as *What's Eating Gilbert Grape*, *Searching for Bobby Fischer*, and *Glengarry Glen Ross*, were critical successes but did lukewarm financially; therefore, there's less of a need for these films, which is another way of saying character-driven stories aren't always commercially viable.

■ The pay isn't as good as it is for plot-driven films.

Chapter Sixteen

Inside Character

I f I've read one book on how to create character in film, I've read a
hundred, and they say the same thing. Certainly these books have
something to contribute to the understanding of how to create a
character. What I've found is that a critical approach to creating
character doesn't work very well for a writer who's sitting in front of a
blank page (or screen). Sure, you can create charts that outline what a
character's outer motivation is as compared to his inner motivation or
how his outer conflict differs from his inner conflict and all that stuff,
but that's too much like trying to make a human being come into being
by cutting out a dress pattern.

It's not that these evaluative approaches don't have some value.
They're great *after the fact*.

So what is it that makes Humphrey Bogart's Sam Spade so compelling in *The Maltese Falcon*? Why is Marlon Brando's Terry Malloy so
electric in *On The Waterfront*? Or was it John Huston's Sam Spade and
Budd Schulberg's Terry Malloy? Who created those characters? The
writers? The directors? Or was it the actors?

Sam Spade and Terry Malloy were a joint invention of all three, but
the writers, Huston (as he interpreted the character of Sam Spade created by Raymond Chandler) and Schulberg, created the raw material
from which the directors shaped and refined the characters. This means,
in effect, that directors and actors are only translators, and their ability
to bring a character to life depends upon their skills as interpreters.
(That *should* mean that film is ultimately the writer's medium, but this
idea doesn't take into account the politics of filmmaking.)

TYPES AND ANTI-TYPES

In an action-driven plot, characters fall into types. Take, for instance,
the lone-wolf male hero between the ages of thirty-five and fifty that

John McTiernan talks about in his interview. Any one of us can list a dozen hero characters that are virtually interchangeable. The equations are straightforward and simple: *Total Recall* could have starred Sylvester Stallone as easily as it starred Arnold Schwarzenegger. *Cliffhanger* could have starred Chuck Norris or Steven Seagal or Jean-Claude Van Damme, and nobody would have cared (except Stallone). What's for sale in these movies is the notion of star power. (Someone once defined a "star" as someone who has two things: charisma, and the ability to sell tickets around the world to a movie that isn't very good.) If you're creating a character that you intend to fit the mold, then you'd better study the mold.

The granddaddy of all action film heroes is Ian Fleming's James Bond. His character type is the basic template for all the lone-wolf male heroes that followed. And since Sean Connery created the first impression of what Bond should look and act like, the other four Bonds that followed (Roger Moore, George Lazenby, Timothy Dalton and Pierce Brosnan) had to emulate the original concept. James Bond is a fixed character: He isn't expected to change or grow in any significant way.

Try to imagine a James Bond who quits Her Majesty's Secret Service and becomes a real estate salesman? Try to imagine a James Bond who falls in love with a plain woman who works in a gift shop in Hertfordshire. Concepts such as interior motivations are almost meaningless. You study the model, and then you emulate it. What matters is the plot.

If, however, you're interested in writing a film that is seriously concerned with the human condition, that wants to explore the recesses of the human spirit and imagination, then you have a different task at hand. As I pointed out in the discussion of character-driven plot, character comes before plot; it is the centerpiece of story. Therefore, it calls for a different approach.

Earlier I talked about playing to character. Playing to character means that you rely on stereotypical notions of types of characters. Let's take on a prevalent and easily recognizable type: the gangster. When Edward G. Robinson played the title character in *Little Caesar* in 1930, and even when James Cagney reprised the character in *Public Enemy* a year later, the stage image of the gangster was startling and brutal. The character of Rico Bandello was original and fresh. In the nearly seventy years that have passed since that performance, not much has changed (with the exception of Marlon Brando's portrayal of the title role in *The Godfather*). As viewers, we're comfortable with and expect that type of character, whether it's in a Scorsese film (*Goodfellas, Casino*) or a B movie. The moves, the tics, the patterns of speech are all the same. The faces change, the names change, but inside the character is the same: They're incarnations of a evolving mythotype of Al Capone. To play to type means that you would create a character that is consistent with the recognizable image of a gangster.

Playing Against Type

To play against type, however, means that you would not only reject the formulated image of the gangster, but that you would create a character that flys in the face of the stereotype. Instead of being heavy set, he would be slight; instead of being brutal and coarse, he would be gentle and refined; instead of being a white man, she would be Spanish. The variations are endless. Sure, we've seen hints of other traits in various gangster films, but they have been slight variations on the same theme. To work against type means a substantial change in the essence of a character. *It means providing the unexpected.*

A plot-driven story relies heavily on type (hence the phrase, typecast). A character-driven story relies on characters who go against type. These aren't people we're used to seeing on the screen. They're fascinating for their individuality; they aren't stock characters taken from the standard menu. In order to create a character that goes against type, you must *know* your character. Most characters in films are one-dimensional, but the truly great characters are three-dimensional. They don't come from the mind so much as they come from the heart of the writer. The writer develops a sense of intimacy with the character: They rise from the page into the imagination. As a writer, you'll identify deeply with these characters; they may even consume you. They aren't disposable; they come back to you over and over, taking on ever-deepening shades of personality. Simplicity gives way to complexity, and you find yourself making an emotional investment in the character.

Goals and Layers

What about motivation? What about conflict? Yes, these are concepts you should be aware of as a writer. Motivation in its simplest sense is what impels a character to act. Why should a character want to do something? Is it out of boredom, hate, love or fear? Don't underestimate the importance of motivation: It is the engine and fuel of the story. Without it, you will have a character who doesn't want or need to do anything. Talk about boring.

So in the largest sense, every character has some kind of goal. Outwardly it can be a simple goal: to climb a mountain, to corner the rice market, to become America's premier ballroom dancer. It is an *objective*. More difficult objectives don't come easily. There are obstacles to overcome. Hence, conflict. If an objective were easy to achieve, it wouldn't be interesting.

Character depth also depends upon more than just surface motivation. Marco wants to become America's premier ballroom dancer. Why? What drives him? This is the pscyhological motive, the deeper impulse that really makes Marco tick. Call it the inner motivation if you want.

My point is that characterization isn't a two-step process: outer motivation plus inner motivation. Character is more like an onion with successive layers. If you're playing to type, only one layer is necessary. If you're interested in exploring a human being and their actions, then you need to go deeper, layer by layer, uncovering complex behavior. In a character-based story, things are rarely what they seem.

So throw away the charts. Character comes with exploration, with delving. It comes because you as the author want to go deeper and understand the nature of this person, not because you have charted and labeled conflicts and motivations.

PRIMARY VERSUS SECONDARY

Individualized characters are wonderful to behold, but they take up a lot of space and time. They are centerpiece characters and they dominate the film. Audience attention is focused on these primary characters, and because you are exploring character as part of the central vision of your screenplay, then you'll have to invest a lot of energy developing that character. Since the average screenplay runs 120 pages (one page of script equals about one minute of screen time) then you don't have the novelistic luxury of taking time to meditate upon the meaning of character. You have to concentrate on doing, not thinking. How do the character's actions reveal their inner self?

As you explore these dimensions of character, you'll quickly realize that you don't have space or time to give all the characters in your screenplay the same kind of depth. While you can (and should) develop depth of character in your primary characters, you might find that you'll have to resort to types for your secondary characters. If you want to write a novel, you can take as much time as you want to explore every nook and cranny of each character. A screenplay doesn't offer that luxury. Everything in a screenplay needs to relate directly to the plot and the motivations of its primary character(s). Stay focused. A good screenplay always cuts close to the bone.

CHARACTER AS ACTION

Henry James wasn't the first to point out that a character is what a character does. It goes back to Aristotle. Even Jean-Paul Sartre in his existential fervor made the point: To do is to be. Whatever your character does reflects on the nature of his or her character. Don't throw your character into action just to keep him busy; action should relate to achieving the primary character's goal, directly or indirectly.

Characters come to life by doing, not by saying. There's a short scene in *Lawrence of Arabia* that gives insight into the main character. The point of the scene is to show that Lawrence is determined to achieve his goal, whatever the personal cost. He harbors an almost pathological fear that he's too weak to accomplish his goal of uniting a fractured Arabia. He's not your typical macho type out to conquer the world; in fact, Lawrence is afraid of any kind of pain. It would be easy for him to sit around with some of his buddies and say, "Gee, fellas, I'm not sure I'm really up to this." Talk is cheap.

The scene in the film is far more intense and doesn't have a single word of dialogue. It's pure action. Alone, Lawrence lights a match and holds it between his fingers until the flame burns him. In the context of the story this isn't bravado. We know Lawrence is afraid of pain, so we understand when he tries to overcome that fear by letting the match burn his fingers. The scene becomes important later in the film, when Lawrence is captured and tortured by sadistic Turks.

Plot, then, is a function of character, and character is a function of plot. The two can't be divided in any meaningful way. Action is their common ground. Without action there is no character, and without action there is no plot.

CHARACTER DYNAMICS

Let's look at how your primary character relates to other major characters. This is called *character dynamics*.

People relate to one another. We can illustrate this with diagrams. When Armand (A) walks into a room and sees Barbara (B) for the first time, he falls in love. Armand asks Barbara out but she tells him to get lost. The story is underway.

The character dynamic here is two. The number doesn't relate to the number of characters directly; rather, it refers to the number of possible emotional interactions: Armand to Barbara (A to B) and Barbara to Armand (B to A).

A -- B

Enter Chuck (C). Barbara lusts after Chuck, not Armand. The character dynamic is now six because of the six possible emotional interactions:

> Armand's relationship to Barbara (A to B);
> Barbara's relationship to Armand (B to A);
> Chuck's relationship to Barbara (C to B);
> Barbara's relationship to Chuck (B to C);
> Armand's relationship to Chuck (A to C);
> Chuck's relationship to Armand (C to A).

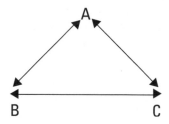

This is the classic *menage a trois*, you can see how the presence of Chuck complicates matters (and makes them a lot more interesting). See François Truffaut's *Jules and Jim* or Paul Mazursky's *Willie and Phil*.

Now add a fourth major character, Darcy (D). Chuck loves Darcy, not Barbara. The character dynamic is now twelve, with twelve emotional interactions possible, because now Darcy has the possibility of interacting with each of the other three characters:

> A to B; A to C; and A to D;
> B to A; B to C; and B to D;
> C to A; C to B; and C to D;
> D to A; D to B; and D to C.

Add a fifth character, and the character dynamic would be *twenty*.

As a writer, you aren't obliged to cover every angle of all the possible relationships. But you'll find that the more characters you add to the

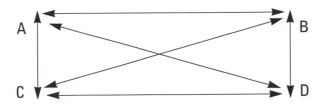

mix, the more difficult it will become to keep up with all of them and to keep them in the action. If you include too many characters, you may "lose" them—forget about them—and when you try to bring them back into the action it will seem forced. Pick the number of characters that you feel comfortable with. That number should allow maximum interaction between characters to keep the viewer interested, but not so many that you feel like you're in the middle of an endless juggling act. The limitations of a screenplay (in terms of time) won't allow for very many character interactions of any depth. Obviously it would be impossible to keep up with the emotional relationships and interactions with a dynamic of twenty. Think of the burden on you as you try to juggle twenty character interactions simultaneously. Juggling twelve is possible, but it takes great skill (*The Big Chill, Enchanted April*). With twelve, you'll have major characters going in and out of phase constantly, with usually no more than three majors in a scene at any one time, except for big confrontation scenes and the climax.

Let's go to the other extreme and look at the original scenario of two major characters with a dynamic of two. We're confined to seeing how Armand acts in the presence of Barbara and how Barbara acts with Armand. This limited situation doesn't offer us the flexibility we need to be comfortable developing their characters. Of course it's been done, and done well, particularly on stage. But having just two major characters limits what you can do with those characters, and you'll need to be a strong, inventive writer to overcome the handicap.

The Rule of Three

Which brings us to the Rule of Three. If you pay attention to the structure—whether it's the classic fable, fairy tale or folktale, or a B movie on television—you'll notice that the number three holds sway. Character *triangles* make the strongest character combination and are the most common in stories. Events also tend to happen in threes. The hero tries three times to overcome an obstacle. He fails the first two times and succeeds the third.

This isn't a secret numerology thing. There's an obvious reason for the power of three: balance. If your hero tries to do something the first time and succeeds, there's no tension in the attempt. If the hero tries to do it twice and succeeds the second time, there's some tension, but not enough to build upon. The third time is the charm. Four times and it's becoming tedious.

The same balance holds true with characterization. Two primary characters are possible in a plot, but it'll lack the wild card character to make things interesting. Three is just right. Things can be unpredictable but not too complicated.

Martin Scorsese's *Casino* works because of its trio of central characters. The character of Robert DeNiro conflicts directly with the character of Joe Pesci. Sharon Stone's character is the wild card, and it's her interaction with the two men that leads to their downfall. Even in apparent two character films such as *Butch Cassidy and the Sundance Kid*, you'll find a third primary character. Three is a comfortable number both for writers and for audiences.

Look at Alfred Hitchcock's *Rebecca* (based upon the novel by Daphne du Maurier). The setup is simple: dark, brooding, and mysterious Maxim de Winter brings home a naive, head-over-heels-in-love bride to his estate, where the memory of his dead wife Rebecca still looms, especially through the character of the housekeeper, Mrs. Danvers, a sinister woman dedicated to the dead woman. De Winter is haunted by his beautiful, dead wife and cannot return the love his new wife lavishes on him. In *Rebecca* the ghost of the dead wife doesn't literally stalk the halls of the mansion but reminders of her are everywhere. The new wife (who has no name in the film) cannot overcome the presence of the old wife. To make matters worse, the housekeeper plots the new wife's destruction.

All three points of the triangle are developed:

1. Maxim de Winter's relationship to Mrs. Danvers and his new wife;
2. Mrs. Danvers' relationship to De Winter and his new wife;
3. The new wife's relationship with her husband and Mrs. Danvers.

Without Mrs. Danvers, the story would've been diminished. She is the antagonist; she keeps the conflict sharp. The new wife wants happiness with her husband; De Winter wants to escape the secret that is haunting him; Mrs. Danver's forces the issue to the front.

Three characters, three acts. The Rule of Three.

Chapter Seventeen

Putting It All Together

At times during the course of the interviews within this book one person will say it's not important to worry about political, social or economic considerations, "Just write the best story you can." The next person says you would be foolish not to take all these meta-fictional dimensions into consideration. So who's right?

One advantage of being the author is that you always get the last word.

I respect the people who I interviewed for this book; they are geniuses of their craft. But they're not writers (with the exception of Tom McGuane and Steven Soderbergh). They have a different point of view—that of director, actor, producer, or whatever. I've heard many prominent people pay homage to writers. Without the writer, they're fond of saying, there wouldn't be a Hollywood. No kidding. That's like saying without chickens there wouldn't be any eggs. Writing is what writers do.

Hollywood knows that. But, Hollywood knows there's no end to the supply of writers willing to queue up to the task. After praising writers, those same people turn around and say with a straight face, "There are no good scripts around, Hollywood is desperate for good scripts."

Hello?

The people who say these things genuinely believe them. In the back of their minds, the writer is both prince and pauper. How easily the writer is praised, and how quickly forgotten.

Sound like sour grapes? Maybe.

My point isn't to complain. I accepted the writer's role long ago, but I'm also realistic. If Hollywood could get along without writers, it would. But that is a prejudice it shares with all crafts. If you intend to become a screenwriter, then you must understand this dichotomous attitude toward writers. You will be held in awe and in contempt; your work is everything, and yet it is nothing. You agree to these terms when you become a screenwriter.

ANATOMY OF A SCREENWRITER

There are three main types of screenwriters. The first kind is the most common. This writer has a story and wants to see it on the screen. It's a precious form of optimism that disdains the odds and believes in the enduring strength of the story.

The second kind of writer has made the investment of time and effort beyond the flush of writing the first screenplay. They've learned rejection but found encouragement at the same time. "Yes, I read your screenplay, and it's very powerful, but it's not the kind of film I want to make. Are you open to the idea of writing a different script for me?" It's a beginning, you say to yourself. You have to make the sacrifices to get started, and so you say "yes" to writing other people's scripts. Sometimes you may even take a job that you don't really like because it puts food on the table, pays the rent, or puts braces on the kids. You develop a cautious attitude, and a touch of cynicism. You feel you're being used, and yet you know you're allowing yourself to be used. Still there's always the fond hope that one day your original script will make it to the screen.

The third kind of writer treats writing solely as a business, not as an art. Work is work. And good-paying work it is. And even though you may be writing for other people, your work may never get to the screen. That's no longer so important. It's a business, and you've gotten good at it. If one of your scripts finally does make it to the screen, all the better: Your asking price will double or even triple.

The majority of writers that get their work to the screen never lose their optimism. They may work for others, but in the back of their head they're still writing their own script. It keeps us sane.

Nor do I bear any grudge against those who'd exploit the system that exploits them. Turnaround is fair play. They're tradesmen, and some of them are very good at their trade.

A screenwriter isn't just a person who writes screenplays. You must learn the intricacies of a craft that borders on the Machiavellian. At times it's exhilarating, and at times it verges on the horrific. You'll know the joy of seeing your ideas, your words and your vision of the world projected on the screen and seen by millions of people. You'll look at Dustin Hoffman or Robert DeNiro or Al Pacino playing a character *you* created, and then you'll look out across the audience mesmerized by the screen and know *you did it*. It's a high that's almost impossible to match.

You'll also know the anger and depression of seeing some of your best ideas discarded, ignored or misinterpreted. You'll know the frustration of not being able to take charge and change things. "Yes, your script is brilliant, thank you very much, and please leave by the side door." And when you're at a wrap party or premiere standing in a room with Gene Hackman and Ridley Scott, everyone's eyes will be on them. You will feel out of place, a stranger at your own party. And yet, believe me, the lows will never compare with the highs.

And, of course, you know all this going in: This is the passage you signed on for.

CONTRADICTIONS

So as far as the contradictory information in this book, let me review some of the suggestions made by the people I interviewed.

#1: Write the best story you know how. Don't worry about anything else.

False. If you were a painter or a poet concerned only for your art and you didn't care what anyone thought about it, then you can afford this attitude. Writing a screenplay is a different proposition. A painting or a poem can exist for its own sake; it has reached its final state. I don't know anyone who writes screenplays and doesn't care whether they're produced or not. The script is unfulfilled as long as it's only on paper. So to say don't worry about "anything else" is to be cavalier.

This attitude suggests that if you write a truly superb screenplay it will make it to the screen, *no matter what*. You hear the same kind of talk in publishing: a truly great novel will get published, no matter what. It sounds good, but no one I know is willing to venture a guess at what constitutes a truly great anything. Greatness is realized after the fact, not before it.

For someone to tell you to "write the best story you can" is meaningless. Of course you're going to write the best story you can. Who's going to write the worst story they can?

Over the years I've read more than a handful of scripts I thought were first-rate, but they never went anywhere, and yet, the local cineplex is raking in the dough with movies like *Dumb and Dumber* and *Ace Ventura: When Natures Calls*. Why is that? Alan Arkin correctly assessed the problem when he said that Hollywood only produces what people want, and if the people want masturbation gags and talking butt jokes, then that's what they're going to get.

Writing the best story you can does *not* mean ignoring the political, social, and economic realities of filmmaking. It means taking into account how the industry works and how it thinks. For the most part the people interviewed for this book don't understand the writing process. You can write the same story as a high-budget extravganza or as a low-budget art film. Knowing how things work makes the difference in *how* you'll write your film.

#2: Leave the details to the experts.

True. As a writer you should never divert your attention from the writer's main task: telling the story. Too many writers get sidetracked by special effects or how to stage the action. Logistics aren't your problem. Leave them to the experts. They have more experience and greater insight into how to accomplish them. Don't offend them by pretending to know better. Furthermore, such distractions interfere with the reading of the story. A script should be pure *what* not *how*.

#3: Camera direction is an important part of good screenwriting.

False. This sentiment was echoed over and over by virtually everyone in the book. Camera direction is the province of the director and the DP. And yet this is the most common problem in screenwriting. Everyone wants to put in his two cents. All you really do is alienate the director and the DP.

#4: Less is more.

True. Avoid writing overly descriptive screenplays. Say in one well-chosen line what you would ordinarily say in three. Sketch, don't illustrate. A common mistake is to overdescribe location and action. Give just enough information so the reader knows where and what.

Some hints:

LOCATION. Where the action occurs is often important. If it's not, then don't waste space on describing it. If it is important, reduce your description to a few critical, well-chosen details. Don't resort to novelistic detail such as:

"Cap Ferat, Cote d'Azur. The bouganivillea are in bloom. Bright reds and yellows splash against the walls of the villa. Across the bay, great white yachts move across the water with the ease of swans. On the terrace, Phillippe sips his Pernod and muses over his previous evening at the bacarrat table."

Screenplay detail can't afford such luxury, especially when the writer's vision demands too much photographically. *Avoid casual detail.*

"Cap Ferat, Cote d'Azur. Phillippe sits on the terrace of the villa sipping a Pernod."

ACTION. The same general rule applies to your description of action. Less is more. If you have a long action sequence, don't try to describe every detail of movement. You want the core of the action, not all the trappings. The likelihood that the sequence would ever be directed just as you describe it is so remote that it's not worth the extra effort. In addition, excess of detail slows down the story.

"Freddie jumps into his blue 1962 Comet, drops it into low gear, and stomps on the accelerator. The Comet bolts forward but it starts to fishtail. Freddie tries to correct, but he's lost control. The Comet veers towards the barn, barely missing some chickens and the dog. Feathers fly. Margie comes screaming out of the house holding a skillet with bacon still sizzling in it."

The core of the action is diluted by all the descriptive detail. Pare it away. Leave one or two details for a little color. Our rewritten version:

"Freddie jumps into the car and stomps on the accelerator. He loses control and veers toward the barn, barely missing some chickens and the dog. Margie comes screaming out of the house still holding a skillet." Same basic action, only told in thirty-six words as opposed to sixty-five. Good description is lean and economical.

CHARACTER. The same rules apply for description of character. Give details that give us insight into the person. Avoid gratuitous detail. We get a strong sense of who a person is by how they look and act. Make external detail a window into the soul.

A description like "His complexion looked like badly set concrete" does a lot more for us than the standard inventory of descriptive details: "He was almost six feet tall with blond hair and blue eyes." Suppose the producer wants to cast Denzell Washington in the role. Six feet tall with blond hair and blue eyes? There's a wonderful moment in *Fatal Attraction* when the character played by Glenn Close is having a small psychotic episode. I don't know if the detail was written into the script, but it's very telling. While she's sitting on the side of her bed staring into nothingness, she mindlessly clicks on and off her bedside lamp. Click, on. Click, off. Click, light. Click, dark. Light. Dark. It's scary stuff. It's also brilliant because it does with action what couldn't be done half so believably with words.

#5: Script format isn't really important.

False. Anything that distracts from the story hurts the reading. The script is a specialized form. Stick to it as closely as possible. By doing that, the form becomes invisible, and the reader focuses all his or her energy on the story. If the format is helter-skelter, then the reader will be constantly drawn away from the story by your homemade version. This is also true for spelling. *If your mispelling words then your divurting attnshun from the story.* You want the reader to concentrate on the contents of the vessel, not the vessel itself.

#6: When looking for an agent, have several scripts available.

True. An agent will be more inclined to take you as a client and more enthusiastic about promoting you if you have a variety of works available. Vary your genres, too. Show that you can write drama and comedy (if you can, of course). Prove you aren't going to be a one-shot writer.

#7: It's better to have a large, well-known agent than a small, less-known agent.

Not always. A big agency might not have enough time to spend on you. It might be too busy servicing its big money-making clients. A big agency will have better contacts, for sure, but if your agent isn't concentrating on you, then having a big-name agency won't do you much good.

On the other hand, a small agency may have the time to spend on you but may not have the same quality of contacts. Be careful what agents tell you when you ask them if they'll be able to give you the time necessary to sell your work. These people are professional salespeople and are trying to convince you that they will have the time and it will be an easy task for them. Put a time limit on their performance: 90 days, 180 days, whatever you feel comfortable with. Don't be too pushy. If you're a pest, they'll dump you. Don't be too complacent either. Visit your agent if you can. Don't make a special trip, but if you happen to be in town, put a face to the name. Your presence also helps spur action.

#8: Once a script has been rejected, it's dead meat.

False. Rejection means, "Not now, not for me (for any number of reasons I can't explain)." Try somewhere else. If you believe in the script, keep it circulating for as long as it takes. *Persistence is the number one virtue for a scriptwriter.* It may take six months; it may take six years. Keep trying.

Another tactic is to constantly change the title of your script. If someone reads your script and writes coverage on it, then it'll be in the computer for others to read. By changing the name, you stymie the system. It helps you overcome what might have been unfair coverage.

#9: You have a better chance if you learn the business.

True. Read the trades. Subscribe to *Hollywood Reporter* and/or *Variety* if you can afford it. If you can't afford it, get your library to subscribe to it. Outside of living in Los Angeles, there's no better insight into the business.

#10: Let your agent take over for you.

False. If you're happy with that kind of arrangement, fine. But you aren't precluded from finding an actor, a director, or a producer by yourself. Be as active marketing your script as you want. Get your script read by anyone willing to read it, from production assistants up to studio chiefs.

OTHER TIPS

1. Always register your script with the Writers Guild before you send it out.

See chapter eleven on how to register a script.

2. Pay attention to production costs as you write.

Common sense is a good rule. Period pieces are very expensive. So are battle sequences or any action that requires a lot of people and equipment. If you're writing for a top-name star, consider their astronomical salaries: Some are in excess of $20 million.

3. Small budget films are easier to sell than large budget films.

Producers keep their eye out for small films that might have a small or limited release (or go directly to video). It's easier to recoup the cost of a low-budget film (under $8 million). Keep your locations simple; keep your cast small; keep your action basic.

4. Think in terms of creating a star vehicle.

You might consider writing a film that would flatter the acting talents of a particular actor. There's always some risk in doing this because if the star you've written for isn't interested, then you might have a difficult time selling it to someone else. Also be careful to avoid writing roles that compete with the main star's. Actors don't like competition.

5. Keep thinking of new ideas.

If a producer should call you in the middle of the night, say he really likes your work, and "Do you have any other ideas?", be ready. Have at least five in your head. Vary them. Keep a notebook with ideas.

6. Polish your pitching skills.

It's not enough just to have ideas. You also need to know how to present them in an interesting and convincing way. Practice the pitch. Keep your presentation down to a minute or two. See chapter nine for details on how to make a pitch.

7. Be persistent.

Never give up.

INDEX

More Great Books
for Writers!

1997 Writer's Market: Where & How to Sell What You Write—Get your work into the right buyers' hands and save yourself the frustration of getting manuscripts returned in the mail. You'll find 4,000 listings loaded with submission information, as well as real life interviews on scriptwriting, networking, freelancing and more! *#10457/$27.99/1008 pages*

Now Available on CD-ROM!

Writer's Market Electronic Edition—Customize your marketing research and speed to the listings that fit your needs using this compact, searchable CD-ROM! *#10520/$39.99*

1997 Writer's Market Combination Package—For maximum usability, order both the book and CD-ROM in one convenient package! *#45148/$49.99*

The Complete Book of Scriptwriting, Revised Edition—Break into the field of scriptwriting as writer/producer J. Michael Straczynski shows you how to write and sell work for television, movies, animation, radio and the theater. Facts, stories and observations from a professional's vantage point will help you make your writing dreams come true! *#10500/$21.99/448 pages*

Successful Scriptwriting—Learn everything you need to know to create and sell your work with this insider's guide to writing and pitching scripts for motion pictures, episodic television, sitcoms and more. Plus, get great marketing advice from heavy-hitters like Larry Gelbart and Steven Bochco. *#10217/$16.99/364 pages/paperback*

The Writer's Essential Desk Reference—Get quick, complete, accurate answers to your important writing questions with this companion volume to *Writer's Market*. You'll cover all aspects of the business side of writing—from information on the World Wide Web and other research sites to opportunities with writer's workshops and the basics on taxes and health insurance. *#10485/$24.99/384 pages*

The Writer's Digest Dictionary of Concise Writing—Make your work leaner, crisper and clearer! Under the guidance of professional editor Robert Hartwell Fiske, you'll learn how to rid your work of common say-nothing phrases while making it tighter and easier to read and understand. *#10482/$19.99/352 pages*

The Writer's Digest Sourcebook for Building Believable Characters—Create unforgettable characters as you "attend" a roundtable where six novelists reveal their approaches to characterization. You'll probe your characters' backgrounds, beliefs and desires with a fill-in-the-blanks questionnaire. And a thesaurus of characteristics will help you develop the many other features no character should be without. *#10463/$17.99/288 pages*

Writing for Money—Discover where to look for writing opportunities—and how to make them pay off. You'll learn how to write for magazines, newspapers, radio and TV, newsletters, greeting cards and a dozen other hungry markets! *#10425/$17.99/256 pages*

The Writer's Digest Guide to Manuscript Formats—Don't take chances with your hard work! Learn how to prepare and submit books, poems, scripts, stories and more with the professional look editors expect from a good writer. *#10025/$19.99/200 pages*

The Art & Craft of Playwriting—An award-winning playwright shares—with energy and smart advice—the nuts and bolts of writing successful stage scripts. From "story" and "tension" right down to how to get a character from one side of the stage to the other, Jeffrey Hatcher conveys his expertise and love of the theater in an intelligent, engaging style. *#48015/$18.99/288 pages*

Make Your Words Work—Loaded with samples and laced with exercises, this guide will help you clean up your prose, refine your style, strengthen your descriptive powers, bring music to your words and much more! *#10399/$14.99/304 pages/paperback*

The Best Writing on Writing, Volume 2—This year's best collection of memorable essays, book excerpts and lectures on fiction, nonfiction, poetry, screenwriting and the writing life. *#48013/$16.99/224 pages/paperback*

Writing to Sell—You'll discover high-quality writing and marketing counsel in this classic writing guide from well-known agent Scott Meredith. His timeless advice will guide you along the professional writing path as you get help with creating characters, plotting a novel, placing your work, formatting a manuscript, deciphering a publishing contract—even combating a slump! *#10476/$17.99/240 pages*

Getting the Words Right: How to Rewrite, Edit & Revise— Reduction, rearrangement, rewording and rechecking—the four Rs of powerful writing. This book provides concrete instruction with dozens of exercises and pages of samples to help you improve your writing through effective revision. *#10172/$14.99/218 pages/paperback*

The Writer's Ultimate Research Guide—Save research time and frustration with the help of this guide. 352 information-packed pages will point you straight to the information you need to create better, more accurate fiction and nonfiction. With hundreds of listings of books and databases, each entry reveals how current the information is, what the content and organization is like and much more! *#10447/$19.99/336 pages*

The Writer's Legal Guide, Revised Edition—Now the answer to all your legal questions is right at your fingertips! The updated version of this treasured desktop companion contains essential information on business issues, copyright protection and registration, contract negotiation, income taxation, electronic rights and much, much more. *#10478/$19.95/256 pages/paperback*

How to Write Attention-Grabbing Query & Cover Letters—Use the secrets Wood reveals to write queries perfectly tailored, too good to turn down! In this guidebook, you will discover why boldness beats blandness in queries every time, ten basics you *must* have in your article queries, ten query blunders that can destroy publication chances and much more. *#10462/$17.99/208 pages*

Writing and Selling Your Novel—Weave the facts and philosophy of fiction to write novels that editors and readers are begging to read. In this completely revised edition, you'll master the art of writing publishable fiction from start to finish as you learn to develop effective work habits, refine your fiction technique and tailor your novels for tightly targeted markets. *#10509/$17.99/208 pages*

Discovering the Writer Within: 40 Days to More Imaginative Writing—Uncover the creative individual inside who will, with encouragement, turn secret thoughts and special moments into enduring words. You'll learn how to find something exciting in unremarkable places, write punchy first sentences for imaginary stories, give a voice to inanimate objects and much more! *#10472/$14.99/192 pages/paperback*